LIBRARY
LOVER'S FUND

Donated by:

Justman
Memorial Fund

FRIENDS
OF THE
PALO ALTO
LIBRARY

In This Together

Also by Ann Romney

The Romney Family Table
Whatever You Choose to Be

In This Together

MY STORY

ANN ROMNEY

THOMAS DUNNE BOOKS

ST. MARTIN'S PRESS 〰 NEW YORK

THOMAS DUNNE BOOKS.
An imprint of St. Martin's Press.

IN THIS TOGETHER. Copyright © 2015 by Ann Romney. All rights reserved. Printed in the United States of America. For information, address St. Martin's Press, 175 Fifth Avenue, New York, N.Y. 10010.

www.thomasdunnebooks.com
www.stmartins.com

Designed by Steven Seighman

All photos courtesy of the author unless otherwise indicated.

The Library of Congress Cataloging-in-Publication Data is available upon request.

ISBN 978-1-250-08397-5 (hardcover)
ISBN 978-1-250-08399-9 (e-book)

Our books may be purchased in bulk for promotional, educational, or business use. Please contact your local bookseller or the Macmillan Corporate and Premium Sales Department at (800) 221-7945, extension 5442, or by e-mail at Macmillan SpecialMarkets@macmillan.com.

First Edition: September 2015

10 9 8 7 6 5 4 3 2 1

*For the more than 50 million people worldwide affected
by neurologic diseases—and for their loved ones—
hope is on the way.*

In This Together

One

MY SON TAGG was working for the Los Angeles Dodgers when Mitt decided he was going to run for president. Tagg enjoyed working for the Dodgers, but he also wanted to come back East to be part of his father's campaign. One afternoon he was talking to the legendary broadcaster Vin Scully and asked for a little advice. "I'm thinking about leaving," Tagg said, then started outlining his plans.

Scully listened for several minutes as Tagg laid out his future, then smiled and grabbed Tagg's arm. "Son," he said, "if you want to make God laugh, just tell him your plans."

I was sitting in a Sunday school class in our church one morning in the early 1990s. We were having a discussion about the various ways people deal with difficult situations. And I remember thinking that many people don't have a huge growth experience until they've had to face a particular challenge. *Wow*, I thought, *my life is pretty good. I'm married to a wonderful and successful man; we have five smart, active, healthy boys; and we're living comfortably in Boston.* At that time, both Mitt's and my parents were alive and they, too, were wonderful people who continued to play important roles in our family life. In fact, as I sat there, I couldn't think of any challenges in my life that had been really difficult to overcome. I took a very deep and satisfied breath. Believe me, I knew how incredibly lucky I was.

The challenges we had faced weren't any different from those of most American families. Raising five boys, we were on a first-name basis with the staff at the local emergency room. We went through all the bloody noses and the broken bones. When our son Ben was ten months old he became ill with what turned out to be a combination of the flu, an infection, and an allergy to penicillin. He was wasting away from something that in earlier times would have killed him. I sat with him for seven days without leaving the hospital as he was treated with IV fluids and eventually got well.

With six men in our house, life often was organized chaos. There was always something unexpected that had to be done right away. It seemed that we were endlessly running from one game to another, from Scout meeting to church event. There was homework to be done and parent-teacher conferences to attend, and there were the everyday problems of five young males racing through childhood and into adolescence that had to be solved. It was a typical family life. We experienced all the cheers and all the tears—and honestly, not everybody always got along. Our two oldest boys, Tagg and Matt, are only nineteen months apart in age, just enough of a difference for them to fight over every single thing. I can still hear one of them complaining about the other one breathing in his space. There was nothing we could do to stop the conflicts. I think every parent at one time experiences that frustration. There were days when I just couldn't take it anymore. I reached the breaking point one afternoon when Tagg was sixteen years old. He and Matt were screaming at each other about some nonsense, and I warned them that enough was enough; they just had to stop. I probably warned them in a pretty loud voice. By then, Tagg was much taller than I, and he turned and started yelling at me. I don't know what got into me; I have never done anything like this before or since, but I just couldn't take it anymore: I hauled off and punched him in the stomach, knocking the wind out of him. I don't know who was more stunned, Tagg or me. Neither of us could believe it. Mitt and the other boys came running from all over the house. Tagg was just looking at me, and everybody else started laughing. My father was in town at that time, and had witnessed this outburst of anger. He looked at me and said, "Oh, Ann, what have these boys done to you?" So, as you can see, rather than being a perfect TV family like the Nelsons, we were just like every other family we knew. We had our ups and, as in this instance, a down.

We also had our family lore. None of us will forget the night one of the boys, who was then four years old, was sleepwalking and somehow mistook our bedroom for the bathroom and our bed for the toilet. Mitt and I leaped out of our bed like it was on fire, while our son simply turned around and returned to his own, completely dry, bed.

We always had a dog, and once we had birds. When Matt discovered six abandoned hatchlings in a nest in a niche in our roof, he decided to raise them. I ended up digging for worms in our backyard, and he fed them to the baby birds. He even taught them to fly, balancing them on his arm and jumping off our rock wall and forcing them to flap their wings. Whenever he played basketball in the driveway, the birds would appear and land on his head and arms. The UPS driver and the mailman got the same treatment. Eventually, though, those birds left our nest.

We also had mice, lots and lots of mice. Our son Josh bought four male white mice for his high school project, although, as it turned out, only one of them was in fact male. For years I had been hoping for more females in our household, but this definitely was not what I had in mind. Within a few months we were raising about a hundred mice in what had been my rarely used sewing room. Inevitably they escaped, and we spent days searching for them in every corner of our house.

While the boys were growing up, we were very comfortable financially, but not wealthy. That came later, when Mitt's company, Bain Capital, became more successful than either of us could ever have imagined. We had gotten married when we both were still in college; we paid $62.50 a month in rent for our tiny apartment in Provo, Utah; we had two folding chairs; our dining room table was an ironing board that folded into the wall; and we were as happy as we could be. While both Mitt's and my parents were successful and affluent, their attitude about life was that you work hard, you don't expect anyone to give you anything, and you live on what you earn. In fact, soon after Mitt and I were married, a large box was delivered to our apartment. It had been sent by my father. When I opened it, I was surprised to see it was a microfiche reader. There was a note attached explaining that he was hoping I might be able to do some work for him in case we needed extra money. Some documents had been damaged in a fire and needed to be transcribed. His way of helping us was providing us an opportunity to work.

Mitt was still in school when our first three children were born, so we certainly needed that money. We saved everywhere we could: We bought the boys' clothes at the Carter's outlet in Boston, I did all the cooking, and I cut everybody's hair myself. Mitt is very mechanical, and he made all the repairs in the house, except for the wiring; he changed the oil in our car and even did our laundry and ironed his own shirts. Our children learned how to work by watching us. It was a joyful time.

Some of our best times together were spent in the dark. As our boys were growing up, fairly regularly each one of them would tiptoe into our bedroom late at night, sit on the couch at the base of our bed, and begin talking about whatever was bothering him. Something about being in the dark, with his brothers asleep and the door closed, allowed each boy to open up to us about his most personal thoughts. We'd talk about problems at school, dilemmas with friends, or hurt feelings. Sometimes, admittedly, I would fall asleep during these conversations, and even Mitt did once—and the strange, contented sound he made instantly became part of our family lore.

While the nature of the problems changed over the years, the custom continued. Still today, when we're together, we go into the family room, turn off all the lights, and talk.

Even after Mitt began earning a good salary, our roles didn't change at all. Our marriage has always been a partnership: His job was putting money in the bank; I was a full-time mother. Being Mom was my job: I cooked every meal, I was the taxi service for five active boys, I cleaned the house. Baseball season was especially tough on our dinner routine; we ate a lot of boy-friendly meals, a lot of spaghetti, tacos, and chicken fajitas. Food has always been the glue in our family; after all, our meals were one of the rare times when we could all be together.

While I felt completely fulfilled personally, I also knew that there were some who judged women who had chosen my path. Mitt was at Harvard Business School, surrounded by type-A personalities chasing success, while I was a stay-at-home mother during the day and attending Harvard extension at night. Mitt and I got married young, but I promised my father I would graduate from college. I knew that those who judged my choices had different priorities from mine; that their happiness came from following a different path. Most important, I knew Mitt completely understood I was working just as hard as he was, but in a different way, and that he valued my contribution to our family. It wasn't just lip service. In every way, he truly considered me as an equal partner.

I so wanted to speak out for other stay-at-home moms, but I just didn't know how to do that. I got that opportunity in the mid-1970s, when the Harvard Business School invited Mitt and me to join several other people speaking about our career choices. Career choices? I had never actually seen it that way. I understood why Mitt had been invited. He was on the path to great success. He was a relatively young vice president of a respected management consulting firm. Only a few years earlier he had sat in that same auditorium as a student and could offer some valuable real-world advice. But me? I had spent those same years changing diapers, burping babies, and making sure our kids got to school on time.

At the time we were asked to speak, we were living near Cambridge, where the feminist movement was in full bloom and motherhood was going out of fashion. There were many people in academia who believed the role of stay-at-home mother, my job, was no longer a viable option for young women. While I had agreed to speak, I didn't have the slightest idea what I was going to say. I would be speaking to students at one of the best business schools in the world, and I knew for certain they weren't spending so many thousands of dollars on tuition so that, one day, they could drive a station wagon and watch *Sesame Street*. Years later, Mitt would describe me as "chief family officer." That was clever, but it certainly wasn't a title that these people were pursuing.

As the day of my speech got closer, rather than being anxious, I became more resolute. Rather than preparing my speech, I decided to be bold; I was going to speak from my heart and talk about the profession I had chosen. Somehow I had to justify the fact that while so many of my contemporaries were shattering the glass ceiling, I was home scraping

Marshmallow Fluff off our boys. As I sat on that stage next to Mitt, watching students stroll into the auditorium, I honestly expected to be booed.

I was the last person scheduled to speak. As the five people who spoke before me explained how and why they had chosen their high-paying occupations, I didn't move. When Mitt finished, the audience applauded politely. Then it was my turn.

"I could have done a lot of different things," I began. "But I didn't. Instead I became a wife and a mother." I turned and pointed at Mitt. "And, by the way, my job's more important than his, because what I'm doing lasts a lot longer than what he's doing." I channeled all my energy into that speech. I hadn't realized just how long I'd been waiting to say these things, and they flowed out of me.

Being a wife and a mother is a complex and physically challenging job, I said. Not only that, it's a lot more difficult than an office job, because it consumes twenty-four hours of every day with no time off. Once I got rolling I didn't hold back. Every child is unique, I continued. Every child is his or her own person, with needs and wants, and no handbook could possibly provide all the information and advice I needed to be a doctor and a nurse, a psychologist, a teacher and a speech therapist, a consultant, a coach, a caregiver, sometimes a boss, and always a friend. I spoke for about ten minutes, which might have been the longest I had ever spoken to an audience.

Finally I concluded: "Mitt and I both know how important his job is. He's the provider, and it's challenging and he's good at it, but we both know that our most important job is raising our kids, and that a lot of that responsibility is mine. And I am fortunate to have a partner that values me as much as Mitt does."

My goal hadn't been to change anybody's mind about their own future; I just wanted a little more respect for women who had made the same choice I had. And whether the audience at Harvard liked it not, I had finally gotten to say it.

As I gathered up my note cards, the applause began—and it grew into a standing ovation. I wasn't used to anything like that, and I probably turned a little bit red. Yet I couldn't spend too much time basking in the recognition—I had to pick up one of our boys to take him to a basketball game and then go home to get dinner ready.

So as I sat in that Sunday school classroom, I knew very well how fortunate we had been to be mostly untouched by the sadness of life. And I was greatly appreciative. But I also understood that there was a natural order to life, and that the only constant was change. Over the next few years, things did change: Our boys grew up, and by the late 1990s only the youngest, Craig, was still living at home. Tagg married, and we became grandparents. Mitt ran for the Senate against Ted Kennedy and lost. Unexpectedly, and certainly without planning, I got pregnant, but in my fourth month, I miscarried. Within much too short a period my parents and Mitt's parents passed away. Mitt and I accepted each of these things, the joys as well as the incredible sadness, as part of the passage of normal life. More important than anything, we had each other and we had our rapidly expanding family. We were settling comfortably into the next part of our lives, ready, we believed, for whatever was to come.

Then I began feeling a strange sensation in my leg.

The symptoms of my disease didn't appear suddenly and overwhelm me. I wasn't attacked. There was no horrendous pain. The initial signs were subtle and easily dismissed. From time to time I'd lose my balance or trip going up a staircase I'd climbed thousands of times. The middle part of my right leg was numb, and that feeling seemed to be expanding upward, into my torso. But the worst symptom, for me, was fatigue, complete and continuous exhaustion. I had always been an incredibly active person: I was a jogger and had run several 5K races; I skied and played tennis regularly; whatever needed to be done I did. It seemed that I never slowed down and I never got tired. But suddenly I could barely get out of bed in the morning. One night Mitt and I were supposed to be at a dinner in Boston and I remember thinking, I don't even know how I can get dressed. The thought of getting in the car and driving into the city to meet Mitt was just overwhelming. I was serving on several boards and committees during this period, and I started skipping meetings.

One afternoon I went grocery shopping with my best friend, Laraine Wright. Our children had grown up together. Our front doors were always opened to each other—which essentially describes our relationship. She was the one person with whom I was so comfortable that there was no need to pretend that everything was fine. Laraine was a nurse, and when anyone got sick or had a problem she always was the first person we called. When it came to health issues, she would know what to do.

That day, while we were out shopping, we walked into the market and I leaned on the cart. I couldn't move. I couldn't even make it down one aisle. It was more than I could deal with. We picked up a few things and left. But if Laraine thought there was a serious issue she didn't say anything.

Still, something was very wrong. Whatever it was, I told myself, it was going to go away. A year earlier I had experienced somewhat similar sensations, and they had subsided. I looked for obvious reasons: I was exhausted because I was trying to do too much. The numbness was probably a pinched nerve. I'd recently had a really bad case of the flu that had just knocked me out. Maybe that was it; maybe I hadn't fully recovered. Everybody loses their balance from time to time. I probably just need a little more sleep—but I got more sleep, and it made no difference at all. I was mystified, I was frightened. I didn't tell anybody, I didn't complain. I felt it had to be something serious, but that was impossible: that type of thing didn't happen to me. It didn't happen to our family. Maybe it was one of those strange flu-type diseases, I told myself, those weird conditions that just seem to hang on forever and then gradually disappear.

I would have gone to a doctor if I had had the slightest idea what type of doctor to see. But I didn't know what I had. It didn't seem productive to tell a doctor, "I just don't feel right. Something's wrong with me." I didn't even know what questions to ask.

The symptoms came and went like a fog: they were there and they would fade. A few years earlier my mother had died of ovarian cancer, and all I could do was watch helplessly. To honor her memory, I joined Massachusetts General's Women's Cancer Advisory Board. One day in 1997, I was walking through the hospital lobby on my way to a meeting when I noticed a pile of pamphlets with the word *diabetes* in bright letters on the cover sitting on a table. I stopped and picked one up. I remember my first thought: *Maybe that's what's wrong with me!* For those few seconds I actually hoped that I had diabetes. That would put a name on my symptoms and allow me to begin treatment. After a few seconds I put the pamphlet back down. No, I didn't have diabetes.

Later that afternoon, I sat alone in my kitchen trying to figure out what to do. I reached for an almost empty glass of milk sitting on the counter—and I could barely pick it up. My brother Jim is an eye surgeon in San Diego. Although we didn't see each other as often as we liked, we spoke regularly on the phone. Along with Laraine, he was my go-to guy for any medical question. "Something's wrong with me, Jim," I explained. "I don't know what it is, but I'm getting a little scared." He listened silently as I told him my symptoms: a loss of balance, weakness, numbness on the inside of my right leg, absolute exhaustion. When I finished, he asked what I thought were random questions about, surprisingly, my eyesight. "Do you have blurred vision?"

"No."

"Pain when you move your eyes?"

"No."

"Do you see colors as vividly as always?"

"Yes."

"Do you have a blind spot?"

"No." These questions seemed silly to me. It wasn't my vision that was bothering me. What I didn't know at that time, and what Jim purposely didn't tell me, was that he was concerned I had something serious and was trying to eliminate some of the early possible indicators. Finally he said softly, "Ann, you really ought to see a neurologist."

I took a deep, slow breath. Once, Jim had been the boy who pulled my hair and told everyone on the school bus I smelled like a barn, but he had become a wonderful, compassionate doctor. The long pause, the soft suggestion, told me he was seriously concerned about me. I didn't understand why I would see a neurologist, but I followed his advice and made an appointment with one of the most respected neurologists in Boston.

Before meeting with this doctor I had an MRI and sent the results to his office. Lying perfectly still in that long tube, listening to the metallic thunk as that machine looked inside my body, I got the first hint that I was about to enter an entirely new world.

Mitt went with me to the doctor's office. Normally I was the one who calmed him down. Within the family, I was known as the Mitt Stabilizer, because I could rein him in when he got too excited or anxious. But as we sat in the waiting room and he held on to my hand, I realized our positions had reversed. Something else had reversed. Six years earlier I'd come regularly to this same hospital to assist my mother with her chemotherapy and radiation treatments.

I'd been the caregiver, the helper. But now I'd crossed that terrible invisible line. This time I was the patient.

I noticed several brochures lying on a table. They were fact sheets about terrible diseases: Lou Gehrig's disease (ALS), brain tumors, Parkinson's, and multiple sclerosis. (There were no fact sheets on pinched nerves or being overtired from too much work.) Both Mitt and I picked some up and began reading. As I read the listed symptoms I realized that some of them were describing me. Mitt's grip on my hand tightened. He knew.

Our reaction was no different from that of the many millions of people who have been in the same situation: This isn't real. This type of thing doesn't happen to us. I remember reading those brochures and wondering whether I had ALS or MS. I kept reading, searching for any symptom I didn't have, looking for some loophole, but there was none.

Eventually we were called into the doctor's office. We knew the doctor socially; his son had attended the same school as our boys. But that day, he was all business. He put me through a series of neurologic tests: While I was seated, he pulled my toe in different directions. Without looking, I was supposed to tell him in which direction he was pulling. I couldn't. He rubbed a key against my leg. I couldn't feel it. He asked me to stand with my feet together and turn around. As I did, I lost my balance and started to fall. I failed every test. The doctor said very little, but it was obvious that each succeeding test was confirming his diagnosis. What is it? I wanted to shout. Tell me! This is my life! Tell me what's wrong with me! Instead, he continued observing my reactions and methodically taking notes. The silence in the examining room was overwhelming.

When he finished, he excused himself, telling us he would be right back. I suspect he was giving us time to absorb what had just happened. As soon as he left the room, I broke down. Mitt cried, too. This was the worst day of his life, he would tell me later, and he began to understand that our life together would never be the same. Eventually he turned and looked at me. "Listen to me, Ann," he said. "As long as this isn't terminal we can deal with it. Whatever it is, we're going to deal with it together."

The doctor returned. Like the cliché jury who returns to the courtroom refusing to look the defendant in the eye because they've found him guilty, the doctor stared at his papers and at Mitt as he started talking about the test results. It wasn't until he was about to deliver his verdict that he looked directly at me. "Ann," he said, "there's no question what we're dealing with here. You have multiple sclerosis."

Multiple sclerosis. MS. I was absolutely terrified. All I could think was, *I'm not even fifty years old, not even fifty years old, and I am never going to have another normal day.* It wasn't precisely a death sentence; he wasn't telling me I had only so many months to live. Instead, in my mind, I was being sentenced to a radically different and severely limited life. My life as I had been living it was over. I was devastated, totally devastated.

Like most people, I knew little about MS except that it was a very serious progressive disease and that after a long period of suffering it could be fatal. I knew one person who had had it: the mother of one of Craig's friends. At one point I had invited her to our house to see some work we'd done and she politely explained, "I'd love to see it, but I don't think I can walk around. It's a little too much for me." I'd been surprised. I was aware that she struggled with fatigue, but I didn't know she lacked the energy to get around the house. When I was given my diagnosis, she was one of the first people I thought about. *That's me*, I thought. *That's my future.*

The doctor showed us the results of the MRI. I heard only bits and pieces of what he was saying. Something about MS being a disease in which your own immune system attacks the protective sheath covering your nerve fibers. He continued talking about this disease, my disease, but my thoughts were racing in every conceivable direction: *What could have caused this? What was going to happen to me? How much time before I felt the full effects of the disease?*

Eventually, I asked the only question that really mattered: What is the best treatment and how soon can I begin? If there was a way of fighting this monster, I intended to do it. I wanted my old life back, and I was ready to fight for it.

There is no treatment, he told me.

No treatment? How could that be? There had to be something.

He nodded. Well, there are treatments, he said, but only when your symptoms get worse. Then they would begin treating me with steroids. But it wasn't time yet, as my symptoms weren't too bad.

Really? I thought. *Not too bad? Try living my life. I can't do anything; I have no energy, I feel terrible all the time, I'm falling, I'm losing the sensation of touch in my body. I can barely get out of bed in the morning. I don't open the mail because I don't have the energy to deal with it. Not too bad? If this is considered not too bad, that means my life is going to get a whole lot more difficult. And I'm supposed to just go home and wait until my symptoms get worse?* I was stunned.

Mitt has always been more practical than I. He's a hands-on person. When something is broken, he fixes it himself. But before he begins, he asks direct, pointed questions and focuses on the details. He likes to learn everything possible, and then figure out what to do. But with each answer he was given, my future seemed bleaker. There was little known about the disease and almost nothing known about how to treat it.

There was one light moment that day. Mitt, looking for some way of reassuring me that we were in this fight together, asked the doctor about intimacy. How does that work, he wondered, and what should we expect? That's a funny thing, the doctor replied. "I've learned that people with MS, they are able to find other ways of expressing their intimacy that can be just as gratifying." Husbands and wives find their own way, he continued, and then told us the story of one couple who found great satisfaction simply by hooking their pinkies.

Mitt looked at him as if he were crazy.

We've been through so much since that moment, but we've never forgotten it. In fact, since that day, sometimes when we're together in a stressful situation we'll grasp pinkies. No one notices it, but that's our way of asking each other in public, "Was that good for you, honey?" However, it took us a long time, on a journey with many twists and turns, to get to that place.

Among the many things I've learned in those years is that my first reaction to the diagnosis, that I was alone in facing it, was very similar to the response of most people diagnosed with a serious disease or suffering after a devastating injury: This is happening to me. Also, I realized that this was very different from anything I had faced before in my life. Not one of the strategies I had developed and applied throughout my life to deal with personal and family problems was applicable to MS. I was facing a monster, and I had not the slightest idea where to begin.

The only suggestion that doctor made was to give me the contact information for an MS support group. Sign up, he urged. But there was no way I was going to do anything like that. I didn't intend to sit back and talk about it. I didn't have the slightest idea where to start or what to do, but simply accepting the inevitable and waiting until my symptoms got bad enough for me to be treated was not an option.

I didn't panic, at least not immediately. I had been taught by my father, a very successful engineer and inventor, a practical man, that panicking did nothing to help or make things easier. His approach, which I had adopted, was to keep a stiff upper lip and *not let anyone else be drawn into this with you*. Then figure it out.

This all took place just before the Internet became such an extraordinary source of information. But as I quickly came to understand, there wasn't much to figure out. From everything I could find, there really wasn't anything I *could* do. All the rule books of my life were gone; all the guidelines by which I had lived were gone. And that's when I felt the first bit of panic.

MS, I learned, is an autoimmune disease in which your own body is actually eating away the insulation protecting your nerves. I imagined it like an army of Pac Men inside me, chewing away. From everything I could determine, the inevitable outcome would be me sitting in a wheelchair, incapacitated, dying young. My life as I knew it was over. There was nothing I could do to prevent it.

Among the very first things we did was tell our family, "We think it's MS." Their reaction was typical and expected: This couldn't be happening. Not to us. Not to our family. And especially not to me. "I hung on to that phrase, 'We think,'" Tagg remembers. "If they just *think* she has it, she probably doesn't, because this stuff doesn't happen to us. I'm sure they're going to find out it's something else and it really isn't a big deal."

It took Tagg and all our children several weeks before they accepted the reality that I really was sick, that this wasn't going away, that all our lives were going to change. There were a lot of tears. When Mitt told his brother, Scott, that I had been diagnosed with MS, Scott broke down. Like us, he knew where this disease was headed.

Besides Mitt and me, it probably affected our youngest son, Craig, the most. At that time he was a senior in high school, the last of our children living at home. He was old enough to be self-sufficient, and was sympathetic and helpful to me, but it hit him hard because everyone at school was telling him that this was really, really bad news. Several of his classmates told him I was going to die. He tried to be brave, and for a while he said nothing about it to me, but it soon became obvious that something was bothering him. Finally we sat down one day and had a conversation. He asked, "Mom, are you going to die?"

"Oh, no," I told him, trying to be more reassuring than I actually felt. "Not from this. Where did you hear that?"

From his friends, he told me.

"Well, I will die one day," I continued, "but this disease isn't going to kill me."

I had to learn how to readjust my own thinking. I had spent my life worrying about my family, but now I had to focus on myself. I didn't go through a long denial phase. I knew something was seriously wrong with me, and as difficult as it was to accept the diagnosis, part of me was glad to be able to put a name on it. At least I knew my enemy.

As anyone who has been in a similar situation knows, the first big fight you wage is against depression. I had an overwhelming feeling of frustration, helplessness, and hopelessness. I was very sick, there didn't seem to be any treatment, and I was getting progressively worse. My mind went to a lonely, dark, very scary place. The disease had made it impossible for me to function, so I would lie in bed thinking about it. I felt like I was on a conveyer belt being carried along and there was nothing I could do to stop it. When I dared look into the future, the only thing I saw was more pain and heartache. Those Pac Men were going to slowly eat away my life. My life was over, I thought. I was never going to have another good day. At the lowest point, in fact, I began wishing that I had a terminal disease that would end my life quickly, because I didn't want to be taken inch by inch. I wanted it to be over.

There was nobody I could talk to about it. I felt more alone than I had been at any time of my life. There was nothing anyone could do to help, and I didn't want to be a burden on anyone.

Mitt tried as much as possible to be optimistic. But we had been together since I was sixteen years old; I knew him much too well to be fooled. When I looked at him, I could see the brave face that he was trying to put on for me. For the first time in our life together, I knew that no matter how upbeat and cheerful he tried to be, he was as frightened as I was. "We'll be okay," he kept telling me. "As long as it isn't fatal, we're fine. If you have to be in a wheelchair, I'll be right there to push it."

And I thought, "But I'll be the one in the wheelchair."

Our friends tried to be supportive, too, offering encouragement and volunteering to help, but there really was nothing they could do. We were told several stories about people they knew who'd had MS and were doing well. And several people believed they had the cure for the disease. We heard a wide range of suggestions; people were convinced that if I ate more of this and stayed away from that, or started taking certain nutritional supplements or tried this elixir or that miracle cure, that I could recover from this thing. Their intentions were good, but they made no difference. As much love and support as people offered, I was in this by myself.

At the same time, there was one thought from which I could draw at least some solace. Several years earlier, Mitt and I had heard an inspiring man named Richard Bushman speak. Professor Bushman was a noted historian then on the faculty of Columbia University, but he also had served as a leader in our Mormon Church in Boston. That day we heard him speak, he told Mitt and me that when he stood on the pulpit looking out upon the congregation, everybody looked so happy. But as he got to meet with these people one by one, he found that every one of them— every single one of them—was carrying a bag of rocks. It might have been anything: a very sick parent, a child with a substance abuse problem, serious financial difficulties. Every one of us, he said, would eventually be carrying a heavy burden, and how we dealt with it would help define our lives.

I had found my own bag of rocks.

Two

WHILE I WAS GROWING UP in Detroit, on some summer nights my father and I would climb up onto the roof of our house and sit there, staring into an endless sky and talking. My father was in awe of the beauty of the universe, but as an engineer, he found the most pleasure in the fact that it was a unified system that worked in predictable ways. There was an order to it. I was about twelve years old when I first heard him talk about God. He was not a religious man, and my two brothers and I rarely had been inside a church; my mother had taken us once, maybe twice, to an Easter service, and I had been completely confused by it. My father did not allow any spiritual instruction in our home. But one evening as we sat on that roof, my father surprised me when he said he believed in the existence of God. There must be a God, he told me, to have created something as beautiful as this earth. But then he added that

God must no longer be involved with the earth, because of all the misery and unhappiness that took place. The evidence of that, he said, was the Holocaust: God could not possibly have watched that happen without stopping it. That was my father's only possible explanation for how a God capable of creating such magnificence could also permit such horror.

After that conversation, I started wondering how the universe worked and if there was a God. I had no one to help me figure it out, no one to answer my questions. In the next few years, I did a lot of reading about the different religions to find out what other people believed—and why. Trying to find out where I fit.

I was just about to turn sixteen when I met eighteen-year-old Mitt Romney. He was a handsome young man, and I was incredibly attracted to him. His father, George Romney, had been the president of American Motors and was governor of Michigan. The fact that the Romneys were Mormon was well known. One night, after Mitt and I had been on several dates, we drove to a secluded spot at the top of a beautiful hill in his sparkling red AMC Rambler Marlin. We were outside the car, just talking, when Mitt finally leaned over and put his arm around my shoulders. When he did, I looked right into his eyes and said softly, "Oh, so you're a Mormon."

That obviously was not what he was hoping to hear at that moment. He nodded.

"What do Mormons believe?" I asked. "I'm really curious."

"We believe in God, the Eternal Father," he said, "and

in His Son, Jesus Christ, and in the Holy Ghost." In very simple terms he explained that his faith gave his life purpose and meaning.

I was struck by that. Obviously I had been searching for something. I was overwhelmed by the simplicity of what he was saying, and it all started to make sense to me. Windows opened and sunshine came in. I felt like I'd found the missing piece of my life. Eventually George Romney baptized me, and since then my religious beliefs have remained very important to me.

So, when I was given this diagnosis, I asked the same question that has been asked at challenging times forever: Why me?

There was no answer to that question. My father eventually concluded that God gave each of us the right to make our own choices, and that the good or the evil things that happened were the result of those decisions. But he also believed that it was up to us to chart our own fates and that little could be accomplished by sitting and waiting. God made the world, but it was up to each of us to make our own way through life. God didn't give me this disease. It was up to me to deal with it.

The day I was diagnosed, Mitt and I went home from the hospital with a brochure about MS that answered all our immediate questions, as if we'd bought a washing machine and had been given a pamphlet outlining its extended warranty. To me, it seemed like a map to nowhere.

As I began adjusting to my new reality, my physical condition got worse every single day. It felt like there was a wildfire raging through me. I would wake up in the morning wondering what part of my body would be attacked that day. The numbness in my leg had started at a spot near my knee; it had now travelled all the way down to my toes and up to my torso. I was starting to have incontinence issues. I tried desperately to fight back as much as I was able. *Keep moving,* I told myself, *maybe if you keep moving it won't catch up with you.* I've always loved swimming, so I went to the pool to try to swim a few laps. I struggled through those few short laps and then went to the changing room. I'd always had such beautiful hair, and taken so much pride in always looking well groomed, but in that changing room, when I tried to blow-dry my hair, I couldn't do it. It was too hard for me. I couldn't hold up the dryer for more than a few seconds. It was a terrible dilemma. The swimming was supposed to have made me feel better, but if my hair looked awful, I would feel lousy about myself. So I stopped swimming. My hair was part of my identity; I couldn't give up my appearance. I was trying desperately to hold on to every little bit of normal life as long as I could.

As much as possible, I tried to avoid thinking about the future, but it was unavoidable. I was starting to accept the possibility that I would very quickly lose the use of my leg, and perhaps even need a wheelchair. Mitt and I were in the midst of building our dream house in Park City, and we went back to the plans to add the elevator I would now need to get from floor to floor. But an elevator wasn't nearly enough: that numbness eventually was going to affect my organs; this disease was going to kill me.

I was neither physically nor emotionally prepared to deal with my symptoms. I tried to learn as much as possible about my enemy. I guess I was looking for the loophole in my diagnosis. I was confident that somewhere in those neatly printed facts in that bright brochure there just had to be some hope for me. It didn't seem possible that after all the advances science had made in fighting once-terrifying diseases that there was no treatment for MS, that the best thing that a fine doctor could offer was to go home until it got worse.

Multiple sclerosis, I learned—and eventually I would learn far more than I'd ever wanted to know—is an auto-immune disease, meaning that my own immune system cells were attacking my body. No one understands why this happens, although there is some speculation that it begins with an infection from a virus that has a structure similar to the cells normally found in the brain, so the immune system attacks both that virus and the healthy areas of the brain. Specifically, it attacks the myelin sheath, the protective insulation that surrounds nerve fibers in the brain and spinal cord and allows the flow of electricity from the nervous system directly to the muscles. By essentially eating away the myelin sheath, MS prevents that flow. Basically, it keeps the brain from telling your muscles what to do. It's like covering the speaker on your phone and trying to talk—some of the information will get through, but not very clearly. Initially the myelin sheath can heal itself, but eventually it loses the ability to make the necessary repairs.

The more I learned about it, the more confusing, and scary, it became. The ability of steroids, at least temporarily, to alleviate the severity of an attack was discovered in the 1960s, although the disease was known for hundreds of years before that. There are written reports of people suffering from similar symptoms in the Middle Ages, although MS wasn't identified as a disease until 1868. That year, Dr. Jean-Martin Charcot, a professor at the University of Paris, who is remembered as "the father of neurology," dissected the brain of a former patient and discovered the characteristic hard nodules, the scars, or plaque, found in MS patients. He therefore named the disease *sclérose en plaques*. Charcot was frustrated that it resisted all the standard medical treatments of that time, including injections of a minute amount of the poison strychnine and even of gold and silver.

It wasn't until 1916 that greatly improved microscopes allowed Scottish researcher James Dawson to describe the effects of the disease in the brain, but the fact that it was an autoimmune disease wasn't known until the 1960s. The development of magnetic resonance imaging in the 1980s allowed scientists for the first time to track the progression of the disease and the effects—or, more often, the *lack* of effects—of potential treatments.

What has always made MS so difficult to diagnose or treat is the fact that the symptoms and progression of the disease are different in every case. Not only is it unique in each patient, but it can even change over time in an individual. That said, we know today that there are two basic categories of MS. The first is progressive MS, where the symptoms proceed without interruption toward greater and greater disability. The other is relapsing-remitting MS, where an attack of symptoms is followed by a remission. The remission does not typically return the person to full recovery, however. Instead, it leaves him or her diminished but temporarily stable. In some cases, relapsing-remitting MS becomes progressive. The great majority of MS sufferers, me included, have the relapsing-remitting form of the disease. A relapsing attack may affect one part of the body, such as eyesight, and then go into remission. Then weeks, months, or years later, it may attack a different part of the body, such as the legs.

Plaque appears in the brain and then disappears. Symptoms will get worse, and then the patient will go into remission. What makes MS so different from other neurologic diseases is that most of them are localized to a single place in the nervous system, while the symptoms of MS appear in many places in the body. And there are a wide range of symptoms, including tremors, an inability to grasp things, tingling and numbness, loss of the use of some or all your limbs, double vision, and even temporary blindness. Rarely, it also can cause personality change: There have been cases in which people become belligerent, hypersexual, or completely uncontrollable. Attacks can come without any warning and can be severe or mild; they can last a few days or a few weeks, or linger for considerably longer; they can relapse or be progressive.

It's sort of the whack-a-mole of diseases: when it is knocked down in one place, it appears in another. It may stay dormant for a while, but then reappear stronger than before. Whatever the course of the disease, however, it is devastating.

When I was diagnosed, I was one of more than two and a half million to suffer from it. It remains the leading cause of paralysis in younger people. It tends to appear more in women than men, and more often in the northern, cooler latitudes than warmer regions. For hundreds of years, scientists have been searching for a vaccine to prevent MS and the other neurologic diseases, or find effective treatments for them. Every time there was a new development or breakthrough in the treatment of a disease, someone would try to adapt it to MS. Jonas Salk, after developing the polio vaccine, turned his attention to MS, but without any success. In a 1978 trial, most of the patients who received his vaccine showed little or no improvement, and in fact, some got worse. Some experiments done on MS over the years have had at least a temporary effect in controlling some symptoms in some patients. Steroids and certain chemotherapy drugs had a positive effect.

As I read this information, I paused and took a deep breath. This was the first glimmer of hope I'd had: a lot of people were studying this disease; there were success stories. But there was no way of predicting what worked for each patient, for how long, or why.

One of the leaders in the research and treatment of MS, a doctor name Howard Weiner, was working at the MS Center he founded at Brigham and Women's Hospital in Boston. Two months after my initial diagnosis, a good friend of ours, Dr. Gordon Williams, a noted endocrinologist also at the Brigham, arranged an appointment for me. In addition to running the MS Center, Dr. Weiner and his close friend Dr. Dennis Selkoe were codirectors of the Center for Neurologic Diseases, which was founded in 1985. (It was called that, I later learned, because the two men decided that using the word *neurologic* rather than the more common *neurological* would catch people's attention.) Like Weiner, Dr. Selkoe, one of the world's leading experts on Alzheimer's disease, had his own center: the Alzheimer's Disease Center. Dr. Weiner and Dr. Selkoe treated patients in their respective centers, but joined to create the neurologic center as an experimental research laboratory. If anyone could do something to help, Gordon Williams told us, it was Dr. Weiner.

The day I walked into his office, I could not possibly have imagined how much both our lives were going to be changed. Dr. Weiner was warm and welcoming, and immediately made me feel that we were in this fight together. As I was to discover, he had spent his entire career battling this enemy and had begun very slowly making progress. Treating MS was not simply his profession; it was his passion.

Weiner was born to be a doctor. His Austrian-born parents had fled Vienna with their families in 1939 and married after settling in Denver, Colorado. His maternal grandfather, Samuel Wasserstrom, had gotten a special visa to leave Austria and was on the passenger ship with his bags when he was taken off. His bags arrived in Denver; he died in Auschwitz. But he had written a letter to his daughter asking her to promise that if she had a son, he could become a doctor. It was an odd request; Wasserstrom was himself a furrier. No one understood it, and in most cases it would have been an impossible promise to keep. But as Howard Weiner once told me, "When I was growing up, I just heard from my mother all the time, 'You're going to be a doctor.' As I got older, when I would walk by a hospital, I actually felt that I needed to be there."

At Dartmouth he was a philosophy major, so when he entered medical school, he decided the brain was our most interesting organ to study and became a neurologist. As a first-year neurology resident at Brigham and Women's Hospital, he remembered, "I took care of a man about my age that had MS. In many ways I identified with him: he had two sons, I had two sons. He'd had an MS attack and recovered from it. There are many diseases that people don't recover from; they just get progressively worse. Alzheimer's disease doesn't stop. Lou Gehrig's disease doesn't go away. But the fact that he had recovered was fascinating for me, because it suggested there are natural mechanisms that can change the course of this disease. So I decided at that time that I wanted to study the disease."

Dr. Weiner experimented with various treatments throughout his career. In the early 1970s, for example, researchers wondered if the disease could be stopped by eliminating from the bloodstream the antibodies that attacked the myelin sheath. In this plasma exchange, which in some ways is similar to a stem cell transplant, plasma is taken from a patient and the toxic factors are removed—in this case, the antibodies would be removed—and then the blood is reinfused. Initially some of Dr. Weiner's patients were afraid to go through this unproven process, so Dr. Weiner went through the plasma exchange treatment himself, to prove to his patients that it was safe. The needle hurt, he remembers, but the process itself caused no problems. Still, while his theory made sense, the results were disappointing.

Yet, as I was about to find out, Dr. Weiner had made substantial progress since then.

In mid-December 1997, Mitt and I were sitting in his office at Brigham and Women's Hospital, desperate for even the slightest suggestion that there was something we could do to help control my disease. Dr. Weiner looked at my MRIs and conducted most of the same tests my first doctor had done. Once again, I failed every test. "Looks like sclerosis has already developed on your spine," he said, confirming the earlier diagnosis. I had MS. Then I showed him the extent of the numbness in my body during that initial visit and how much it had progressed in the ensuing two months. He listened silently as we told him what my first doctor had said, but I noticed that when I told him we had been advised to go home until my symptoms got worse, he shook his head in disdain. I took that as a positive sign.

We asked him many of the same questions we had asked the first doctor. His answers were pretty much the same, but the cautiously optimistic tone in his voice somehow made them less frightening.

The one thing he could not do was predict the path of my disease.

"What should I expect?" I asked.

"The unexpected," he said, although those weren't his precise words. The insidious thing about MS was its unpredictability, he explained. This is what made it so different from other neurologic diseases. And while some progress had been made in understanding the cause and course of MS, there still was no way of knowing how it would affect a given patient. He told us about several of his patients who, with just a little assistance, had been able to lead almost normal lives.

Finally, he told us that while treatment remained an inexact science, waiting was not one of the options. "What they're telling you is crazy," he said. "We've got to knock this thing down. I can't tell you we can cure it, but we can treat it." He told us that I had relapsing-remitting MS, although it was progressing very rapidly. My experience with the disease was not unusual. Once the relapsing type strikes, it can move through your body very rapidly and result in severe disability. The most important thing to do was blunt that initial attack to prevent the loss of motor function. If we didn't stop it very quickly, he continued, it could lead to significant and permanent disability. Dr. Weiner proceeded to tell us about several different strategies he had used, sometimes very successfully, to help other people with this form of MS. Then he stood and offered me his hand. "We're going to attack it and we're going to start right now," he said. "Come with me."

I was stunned. I almost burst into tears. There was no equivocation in his voice: *Come with me.* Those words offered the first real hope that there was some way of fighting back.

Dr. Weiner literally led me by the hand down the hall into what is known as the infusion room. There were several other men and women in the room, sitting quietly with needles in their arms as some liquid dripped slowly into their bodies. While the fact that we were taking the offense gave me comfort, as I looked around the room I became terrified that I was looking at my own future. Most of these people were in wheelchairs, several of them with bladder bags hanging from the sides.

I sat down in an infusion chair, and a nurse-practitioner came over and sat next to me. Apparently she had seen the fear in my eyes. She patted me reassuringly on my arm and whispered, "Don't be too concerned about all these other people. Everybody's response to treatment is different. This doesn't mean you're going to have to be this way." Be positive, she continued. Be cheerful; you're going to be okay. I heard every word, and I tried to believe her. And a little of me did believe it might not be as terrible as I thought. But as I looked around I saw pretty graphic evidence of where this disease can take you.

Dr. Weiner explained his strategy to me: Hit it early, hit it hard. Don't let it take root. He was blasting my body with a steroid, cortisone, one of the drugs most commonly used to fight MS. For some people it worked amazingly well, for others it had no effect. Doctors did not yet understand the reasons for this. When I asked him why my first doctor hadn't tried this, he didn't have an answer. MS is a disease for which there is no standard treatment protocol, he explained. In many ways, treating it is an art. He suggested that the difference in approaches might be due to the fact that in the past many of the neurologic diseases couldn't be treated, so the profession attracted people who liked to diagnose it, think about it, research it, and do anatomy, but who did not have the same treatment culture as other medical disciplines.

That just wasn't him, he told me, and then he quoted King Lear's wise advice, "Nothing will come of nothing."

In the early 1980s, Weiner had performed a series of experiments treating MS patients with chemotherapy and had discovered that "strong modulations in the immune system could make a big difference in the outcome." Steroids had been commonly available before and had been used successfully to treat patients to combat especially bad attacks, but they hadn't been aggressively used to fight the disease in its early stages. As Dr. Weiner explained, "I applied that idea to using known therapies and not being afraid to use them to shut down a person's disease." He believed in attacking the disease with every weapon available, as quickly as possible. For many patients, but not all, it worked.

It worked for me. The numbness began receding—so slowly at first that I wasn't certain it was real, but as the steroids took hold, the numbness receded all the way back down my leg, where it stopped. *Oh my gosh*, I thought gratefully, *there's a chance I can have my life back*. For the first time I knew that I had a weapon to fight back. Oh, how I hated those steroids—the side effects were devastating—but they meant that, at least temporarily, I could keep the monster at bay. It wasn't a cure. My leg was still weak and numb, but I could live with that. The numbness was localized, and I could live with that. It was just so hard for me to accept the unrelenting extreme fatigue that had become my new reality. I felt like I was living in a fog, and worse, that I had become a burden.

The actual infusions took about an hour. The process is very much like chemotherapy: you relax in a chair while hooked up to a machine that slowly drips a liquid from an

IV bag into your vein. Some people read. I couldn't; my mind was too unsettled to concentrate on anything. I just sat there by myself looking around the room incredulously, wondering how in the world I had ended up there. I had walked into the hospital on my own two feet, but looking at those people in their wheelchairs, I wondered how much longer I would be able to do that.

I would drive back and forth to these treatments by myself. Mitt always offered to go with me, practically insisting on it, but I wouldn't let him, telling him, "No, absolutely not. I'll be okay." I was trying desperately to hold on to whatever independence I had left. I was trying to be as tough as my father would have been. I didn't want to show the slightest vulnerability or fear, or let anybody see the turmoil boiling inside. In the infusion room, I kept very much to myself. That room is a very public place to have such an extraordinarily private experience.

I knew the steroid was poisoning my body, but that was the price of hope, and I was willing to pay it. Cortisone depletes your calcium, weakening your bones. So I would bring a bottle of Tums with me, because they contain an abundance of calcium. Then I would sit in my infusion chair with a fluid going in my veins taking *out* my calcium while madly chewing Tums trying to replace it. I knew it made no sense, that it was useless, but it made me feel I was doing something, anything, to fight back.

Since the onset of my symptoms, my attention had been focused entirely on my health. I hadn't really given much thought about the effects of my diagnosis on anybody else. I guess I began to understand how my illness was changing the dynamics of the family when we all gathered in December 1998 to celebrate Christmas. I don't think any of my children truly understood the seriousness of my illness until then.

Christmas was my favorite time of the year. We had a lot of family traditions. During the holidays, my job included doing everything. The holiday wasn't a chore for me; it was my choice, and I leaped happily into it. I loved putting up all the decorations. I loved having everybody home, and buying and wrapping presents. I loved stuffing stockings, and I loved cooking big meals in a warm, crowded, noisy kitchen for our whole family. I looked forward for weeks to skiing with our children and sledding with our grandchildren, and to putting the babies to bed with Mitt and then sitting with him and our boys and their wives in a dark room late into the night as we caught up on all their lives.

So it was shocking to everyone when I could barely get out of bed. There have been very few moments in my life as depressing as lying in bed listening to the subdued chatter of an active family as they each did their best not to disturb me. I tried as much as possible to fulfill my traditional role, and everyone joined me in this pretense. At times the house seemed normal: the lights on the tree were blinking colorfully, the kids were playing downstairs, the boys were involved in some kind of card game, and the music of Perry Como drifting through the house was reminding all of us that there was no place like home for the holidays. But I didn't have the strength to be part of it. I wanted so much to be part of our family celebration. I wanted to contribute, to be Mom. I couldn't. This disease was taking everything away from me. I felt so completely left out; the world was going on without me.

Everyone took turns coming into the bedroom room with forced enthusiasm, but we were all living under a thick layer of pretend normalcy. Nobody dared say what was so obvious. We celebrated the entire holiday in denial, perhaps trying to squeeze in just one more family gathering before whatever was coming next. It might not have been so terrible if I'd believed that it was temporary, that it was simply an inconvenient and depressing step toward a better, healthier life. But I knew that it wasn't temporary, something that would pass like a bad cold. This was my new life.

We had never celebrated a family Christmas without me being in the middle of everything, and everybody tried to pick up the slack. They shared the cooking and the cleaning. Mitt organized the kitchen and actually did some of the cooking. Things got done, but the joy was missing. I tried. I tried so hard. One morning as I lay in bed looking up at the ceiling, I realized I hadn't gotten a present for Josh. He didn't need anything and would have understood completely, but I became fixated on that. It became symbolic of everything I was no longer able to do. When I finally told Mitt what was bothering me, he immediately took charge. "Then let's go," he said. "Let's take care of it."

He helped me into the car, and we drove to a sporting goods store. For a few moments everything was okay: Mitt and I were going shopping for one of our boys. But when we got to the store I realized I just didn't have the energy to swing my legs out of the car. Walking inside and shopping was completely impossible. I sat in the front seat, feeling utterly defeated, and watched Mitt enter the store. *He doesn't have the slightest idea what he's doing*, I thought, but I loved him so much for his effort. A few minutes later he came back happily swinging a bag.

Our roles had been reversed. "Everything's getting done," Mitt said proudly later, sitting down on the bed next to me. I had no bravado left in me. I tried to explain to him how closely *what I did* was tied to *who I was* in the family, but Mitt thought that was preposterous.

"Sweetie," he said softly while stroking my hair. "You know that I appreciate everything you do to make Christmas so special for everyone, but that's not why I love you." His next sentence gave me the small dose of hope I needed right at that moment, its simple absurdity striking me to the core. "And I certainly don't love you because you make the dinners."

He sat there gently stroking my hair as I closed my eyes and fell asleep.

Mitt had always been wonderful in a crisis. He took action. Once, in the mid-1980s, when we were living in Belmont, Massachusetts, the young son of close friends was playing with matches underneath their basement Ping-Pong table when it caught fire. The boy was running up and down the stairs with glasses of water from the kitchen trying to put the fire out. His father asked him what he was doing, and he said it was nothing. Then his father smelled the smoke. The entire house went up in flames. Mitt got there before the fire department, and ran in and out of the house many times to help save whatever important possessions he could.

This family moved in with us for several weeks until they found a place to stay while their home was being rebuilt. They stored their possessions in our basement—which is where they were when our dryer caught fire! Fortunately, Mitt had made sure all of our fire extinguishers were working, and we quickly put out the flames.

But MS was the kind of crisis even Mitt couldn't do anything about. There were no actions to take, no fires to put out. It wasn't that easy.

I was slowly beginning to accept the fact that this was a life sentence. For a while I would go to sleep at night hoping I would wake up in the morning feeling wonderful and realizing that it had all just been a bad dream. But when I woke up the next morning, I wouldn't feel wonderful. I have always been a person who likes to charge into the day. Yet now I would lie there wondering how I was going to get through it. Among the many changes that had taken place in my life, this was the first time I really had nothing to look forward to. Later I would find out that these feelings are typical of people diagnosed with a chronic illness or suffering a life-changing injury, and that there are different ways of dealing with it. For me, the beginning of that understanding was a phone call from someone I didn't even know.

The call came unexpectedly—which is how so much in life happens—from a friend of a friend. This woman was about three years more into the disease than I was, and wanted to share what she had learned. "Look," she practically ordered me, "go get a pen and some paper and start taking notes 'cause I'm going to tell you all the things you're going to go through and all the challenges you're going to have. And then I'm going to give you some solutions."

I got a pen and paper and listened. "You've basically moved into a new body," she began. "The things you took for granted before are no longer true anymore, and it's your job to take care of this new body. You have to listen to it and pay more attention to it than you're used to doing, and you have to understand and accept the fact that you have limitations. This first year is going to require a huge, huge adjustment." The metaphor for this new reality is the gas tank in a car. I'm not sure if she told me this or if it's a conclusion I reached, but it goes like this: Every car has a reserve tank, so even when the fuel gauge indicates empty, there is a little extra in there to enable you to get to the next gas station. But with MS, when you run out of gas, there is no reserve. You simply stop short. So you want to stop well before that point, when there are still fumes left in the tank. I would learn this later, as I determined how far this new body of mine would go on what I had left inside. "You can't go out at night," she continued. "You have to be in bed. On most days by three o'clock in the afternoon, you're done. People are going to try to push you a little, because you don't look any differently to them. They can't see your new body, so they think they're doing you a favor. They're not, and the people who love you most have to understand that you're not who you were before and can't do the same things." Things will change, she promised, as I learned how to conserve my energy and recognize and adjust to the warning signs. "Learn your limitations," she said.

Then she began talking about alternative therapies. This was the first time anyone had suggested these. I have complete trust in Western medicine, and for the most part, I had never been too interested in or knowledgeable about holistic treatments. What I had read about them didn't seem to make much sense to me. Some of them seemed pretty way out there. But this friend of a friend opened my eyes to the possibilities of holistic treatments when she said flatly, "There are things out there that will make you feel better."

While I had my doubts, I wrote down everything she told me. One of the treatments she mentioned doing was something called craniosacral therapy, which I had never heard of. It's a type of gentle manipulation that balances the fluids in your brain, she explained. It was a relatively new treatment and hadn't been studied extensively. A lot of medical doctors thought it was nonsense, and told her that she was wasting her money—except that it worked for her. Then she told me about reflexology, which involved applying pressure to the hands and feet. It sounded a little like acupuncture to me. I didn't make any judgments; I just wrote it down.

She told me about several other equally novel treatments that other people she knew had pursued. Some of them had made no difference, but others had resulted in some success. Normally I would have dismissed all this as some sort of hocus-pocus, but there was no longer any normal for me. I was desperate, and willing to try anything that offered the slightest promise of help.

That phone call made a difference to me. While this woman's advice and information was to prove very valuable to me, far more important was her underlying message: While she never said it directly, her larger point was that I wasn't alone. So many other people had faced the same challenges and overcome them—she, for one—and had moved forward to live complete and productive lives.

She was the welcome wagon to the rest of my life.

At first I wasn't sure what to do with this laundry list of lessons. When I reread my notes and saw words such as *craniosacral* and *reflexology*, I took a long, deep breath. Probably more than at any other time during this period, I really missed having Edward Roderick Davies, my wonderful and eccentric father, to turn to for advice. Many of the other people I knew probably would have advised me to forget about all that hocus-pocus and rely on the miracles of science, but not my father. He was a man who embraced all the possibilities of the world. He was a student of nature and all its complexities. He still is the only man I've ever known who got really excited when the new issue of *National Geographic* arrived, and he'd read it from cover to cover—and then insist on sharing the knowledge he'd gained. Until the end of his life, he was curious about absolutely everything, from the minutiae of his grandson's homework to the way to make a more efficient ski lift.

No problem fazed him. I remember the day my brother Jim brought his future wife, Becky, to our home in Bloomfield Hills, Michigan, to meet our parents. Within minutes of her arrival, my father had her standing in the bathroom holding an eight-foot-long strip of toilet paper. The other end was in a strange-looking toilet. I've never seen anybody so excited about a toilet as my dad. The vacuum toilet was a prototype for his latest invention for the navy; it got rid of waste without wasting water. When he flushed it, the paper disappeared almost instantly.

My father's curiosity never diminished. He died in 1992 from something called a hemangiosarcoma, a fast-growing cancer. As I sat with him in a hospital in Stuart, Florida, saying good-bye, I remember the final advice he gave me: "Ann, I'm so excited for you because you have so much ahead in life. Don't be afraid of anything." And then he said, "I'm so sad to be leaving this world because there is so much more to learn. I hate to miss it. I can't imagine the explosion of knowledge that's going to happen, and you're going to be there to see it. Please make the most of every opportunity."

I couldn't ignore my father's words: don't be afraid of anything. So rather than simply following the path laid out for me by Dr. Weiner, I eventually decided to explore other possibilities. But I didn't say anything about that decision to Mitt. Not yet. I was quite sure he knew no more about craniosacral therapy than I did.

One point that this friend of a friend made that was difficult for me to embrace was that I had to accept the realities of my new life. For me that meant not just letting people help me, but also asking for help when I needed it. I wasn't good at that. In fact, I've found that few women are. We take such pride in being caregivers, seeing to the needs of our families, that sometimes we forget how to ask for help when we require it. I never thought of myself as Superwoman, but I persisted in doing all the chores around the house, including cleaning, for a long, long time after we easily could have afforded help. That was my choice. It was difficult for me to accept the reality that I couldn't do those things anymore, that I needed to learn how to depend on other people.

I fought it at first. For most of my life I'd found my identity in being a caregiver. I was the woman who stood up and told a Harvard Business School class that being a mother and homemaker was a full-time job. And I drew great satisfaction from it. So in addition to my new physical limitations, admitting that I could no longer do all that meant a loss of identity for me. That was a difficult psychological hurdle to overcome. My family did everything they could to mitigate this. I knew they loved me unconditionally, but I was in a truly dark spot. Who was I now? I was a person who could not get out of bed. I was a burden.

This is where Mitt stepped in. At my lowest, darkest hour, Mitt pulled me out of that place, saying, "Your worth is not what you do; it's who you are." His love for me was overwhelming, and not based on the things I did. He loved me for who I was. His love allowed me to let go of that old identity. Certainly one of the most important lessons I learned as I began to live with this disease was that I couldn't fight it alone. Nobody can. I was going to need help, and I was going to have to ask my husband and my family and my friends for it.

I turned also to my friend Laraine Wright. Laraine and I had always been each other's biggest cheerleaders; we were always there to cheer each other on. I had first turned to her because of her medical background. When I was diagnosed, she immediately told me, "We need another opinion." Her brother, she reminded me, had once been told he had MS, but the diagnosis turned out to be incorrect—he eventually was diagnosed with post-polio, meaning he was relapsing from a childhood case. He was several years ahead of me, too, so Laraine had already been through so much with him.

Laraine immediately fell into the role of my caregiver, although I didn't recognize it right away. My fear was that I would become a burden on my family, so there were things I didn't easily admit to them. But from the very beginning, I dumped everything on Laraine. I didn't hide anything from her. One night in early January, I was feeling a little bit better and was desperate to get out of the house. I had tickets to a symphony and asked her to go with me. It was a wonderful evening, and for a time, I was able to forget about my illness and live happily in the music.

After the concert we started walking to the parking lot and I felt all my strength drain out of me, almost as if someone had just pulled a plug. I was dizzy and having a difficult time standing. Getting to the car by myself was impossible. "Laraine," I said, "can I hold on to your arm, please. I'm losing my balance and I need some help."

I need some help. It was harder than I thought to say those words. Asking her medical questions was easy; I'd been doing that for many years. Talking to her about my frustrations and my fears wasn't especially difficult; we were as close as sisters. We'd been through so much together. When Mitt had entered politics in 1994 and run for the Senate against Ted Kennedy, Laraine was with me for all the good days and the last final sad day. When my parents were dying, she was understanding and sympathetic. Emotionally, she had been there for every chapter of my life—but this was different. This was an admission of my vulnerability.

Laraine put out her arm, and I took hold. My eyes welled with tears and when I looked at her, she forced a smile and then turned away. She didn't want me to see her tears. She helped me back to the car, and I sort of collapsed into the seat. We didn't speak the whole ride home.

After that I was able to open myself up and allow other people to provide whatever assistance they could, whether physical or emotional. Within a few years, I would become the person on the other end of the phone, talking to people newly diagnosed with MS or other debilitating diseases, or to people who were recovering from serious accidents. I would do my best to reinforce the fact that this was not the end of their lives. I would provide encouragement and tell them about the lessons I had learned. And I would tell them about my caregivers, my family, and my old friends, and all the people who came into my life directly because of my disease and made such a tremendous difference. Some who came into my life as caregivers have subsequently become close and long-lasting friends.

So much had changed in such a short period of time. Reluctantly, very reluctantly, I found myself at the beginning of a new and unexpected life. So I set out to explore all the possibilities. After all, I was my father's daughter.

Three

ANY LIFE-CHANGING EVENT also changes all your relationships. It isn't just you who has to learn to adapt; everyone else has to learn how to deal with the new normal. Only after I began to accept my diagnosis, and my initial depression began to lift, did I begin to understand how incredibly fortunate I was. I know how lucky I am. Unlike many other people who are suddenly faced with a significant challenge, Mitt and I had the resources to do whatever was necessary. But more than that, I had a husband who loved me unconditionally, who always put my needs before his own.

During the 1994 U.S. Senate race, I told an interviewer that Mitt and I had never had a real fight. This was such an unusual claim to make that most people believed that either we weren't being honest with each other or I was saying it for political purposes. But it is absolutely true. We've certainly had our squabbles, we've gotten frustrated with each other, but we don't fight. I like to believe that Mitt knows how fortunate he was to get me (!) and he doesn't want to rock the boat.

The fact that we don't fight is sometimes comical. In the late 1980s, I bought Mitt a used BMW for his fortieth birthday. That car is still in the family, and he loves it. He has always treated it with great care; it was one of those cars that he would use only when the sun was shining. Unfortunately, I drove the car one day and left the sunroof open; I forgot all about it. Naturally it rained that night; it rained a lot. In the morning I was in the kitchen with the boys when Mitt came storming in. There were about four inches of water in his car. He was so angry that smoke was coming out of his ears. "Who did it?" he said to the boys. "Which one of you left the sunroof open?"

The boys looked at each other, assuming one of their brothers had done it.

I said, "Oh gosh, it was me. I'm so sorry, Mitt."

He looked at me and said brightly, "Oh that's okay. It'll dry out. We'll take it in and get it fixed."

That basically sums up our relationship. But it isn't one-sided. I feel the same way about him. So when I got a phone call asking if I would agree to another significant change, a change that would force us to uproot our lives, I agreed almost immediately.

In late January 1998, about two months after my diagnosis, I received a call at home from Kem Gardner of Salt Lake City, Utah. We had come to know Kem several years before, when he served as president of our church's missionary program in Massachusetts. In the Mormon Church, most young men and many young women voluntarily serve two-year missions to share our faith with others. Missions are also a growing experience for these young people, the concept apparently being that maturity increases with every door slammed in your face. Because Mitt held several leadership and pastoral positions, he and Kem frequently worked together, and had become fast friends. After his stint in Massachusetts, Kem had returned to Utah to resume his successful business as a real estate developer.

Kem's call was about the Olympic Winter Games, which were scheduled to be held in Salt Lake City in 2002. I already had heard that the Games were in serious trouble as a result of a scandal that had shaken the Olympic world. The media reported that Salt Lake's Olympic organizers had made large payments and gifts to members of the International Olympic Committee in order to win the bid to host the Games. It looked and sounded like bribery. Some said that the Olympics should be moved elsewhere. Furthermore, the FBI was investigating to see whether the Salt Lake organizers had violated federal law.

Kem explained that someone from the outside, someone with unquestioned integrity and unmatched capability, was needed to come to Utah to get the Olympics back on track. In Kem's mind, that someone was Mitt. I asked him why he was calling me instead of Mitt. "Because I know that if I call him," Kem said, "he will just say no. But if you're convinced, you'll be able to convince him too."

I've lived a lot of my life based on what I feel in my heart. As soon as Kem finished making his pitch, I felt it was the right thing to do. This was something important for the country, for the state where Mitt's parents had been raised, for the American athletes who had trained for years, and for the Olympics in general. I also knew that this would not be an easy decision: we would have to move to Utah and give up Mitt's compensation from Bain Capital. But it had been obvious to me for a long time that Mitt was going to need a greater challenge; he would never be happy in life just making money.

As I was my father's daughter, Mitt was his father's son. George Romney was a remarkable man. He had been a tremendously successful auto industry executive, but quit that job to enter public service. He became one of the most popular governors in Michigan history, a leader of the civil rights movement, and a very strong contender for the Republican presidential nomination in 1968. Eventually he served as President Nixon's secretary of housing and urban development, where he became a champion of fair housing. After leaving government, he served as head of the National Center for Voluntary Action for almost two decades. So Mitt had a compelling model of dedicated public service to follow.

A job like this fit him perfectly. We were just finishing building our dream ski house in Park City, which was not far from Salt Lake. Even the towels were there, so we could move right in. But after my initial reaction to the Olympics idea, I paused and looked at reality: How would I be able to handle it? Dr. Weiner, my family, and my growing support group were all in Boston, a long flight from Salt Lake City. I wasn't certain how much time I'd physically be able to spend out there, and neither Mitt nor I do especially well when we're separated for long periods of time. And Mitt had already taken an extended leave of absence from Bain, when he ran against Ted Kennedy. It wouldn't be fair to his partners to do it again; if he accepted the offer, he would have to leave Bain permanently. Besides that, our youngest son, Craig, was completing his senior year in high school and we certainly weren't going to take him away from his class and friends.

Realistically, it didn't make a lot of sense. But that just wasn't how Mitt and I made our decisions. Many years earlier, Mitt had to decide whether to go on a church mission, as his grandfather, father, and brother had done. Normally it would have been an easy decision to make, but by that time, Mitt and I were deeply in love. We were still teenagers, though, and most teenage romances don't survive extended separations. When his father was in a similar situation, he asked the woman who later became his wife, Lenore, to promise never to kiss another man. As she later said, "I kept that promise, but it took some fancy footwork . . . One boy did kiss me, but I didn't cooperate!"

Mitt didn't want to risk our relationship, so he decided not to go on mission. I insisted that he go, telling him, "If you don't you're going to regret it for the rest of your life. And I don't want to be part of that." After that, he did go, and of course our relationship survived. That experience taught us the benefits of taking risks. Neither one of us wanted to live our life with regrets about those things we hadn't done. At the end of our lives, we didn't want to have to look back and wonder how differently things might have been if we'd taken the riskier path; we didn't ever want to have to say the two saddest words in the English language, *if only*.

If I had told Kem we wouldn't be able to accept the Olympics job, and had hung up the phone, Mitt would never have known about this phone call. While I couldn't be sure Mitt would accept the offer, I wanted him to make that decision. When I called him at his office, he responded exactly as I would have guessed: "That's ridiculous," he said. "I would never do something like that."

Well, Kem had been right so far: Mitt would immediately reject the idea out of hand. But I didn't give up. "I think we should do it," I said, "and I don't want you to say no without giving it a lot more thought and without more time to talk it over." Mitt reluctantly agreed.

I knew how hard a decision like this would be for him. He had spent over ten years building a successful company, and taking the Olympics job would mean walking out the door for the last time. He would be leaving Bain Capital behind just as it was poised to become much larger and even more lucrative. He'd be stepping into a turnaround where the consequences of failure could be severe and very public.

We made a trip to Utah and met with Governor Leavitt and several other board members. Like Kem, they were convinced that Mitt was what the Olympics needed. Our ultimate decision was the result of our growing appreciation for what the Olympics meant: The Games are one of the few things on the world stage where young people see the great qualities of the human spirit. They see dedication, teamwork, sacrifice, hard work, determination—all these and more are displayed day after day in homes across America and around the world. We felt it was important that the Games succeed, and we believed that Mitt had the experience and skills needed for that to happen.

We gave a great deal of thought to how this decision might affect my health. Mitt said that if taking the Olympics job would exacerbate my MS by even the tiniest amount, we would turn it down. We spoke with Dr. Weiner. He assured us that he would direct the treatment I would be given in Salt Lake. In some ways, we wondered whether walking away from all my responsibilities in Boston might actually improve my condition, not hurt it. I was too tired to serve on my boards, too tired to drive around Boston looking for a place to park, and too tired to keep up with all my friends and activities. In Utah, I would have fewer responsibilities and I would be living in a beautiful, peaceful place.

It was a go. We discovered pretty quickly, however, that this was going to be a great deal more difficult than we imagined. I had been to Park City many times, but that was before I was struck by this disease. In Boston the changes had been gradual; each day, I was able to do a little less. But when I got to Park City, the toll my disease had taken was obvious. I was a different person from who I'd been the last time we were there. Things I had done countless times without ever thinking about them suddenly became obstacles. Park City is built on the side of a mountain. Walking up Main Street really means walking uphill. I remember standing at the bottom of the street and thinking, *Whoa, I can't do this. This is just too much for me.* I even lacked the strength to make it just once around the block.

Meanwhile, Mitt was surprised to discover that the Olympics situation was much worse than he had anticipated. The Games were running a deficit of $379 million. The federal government was balking at providing transportation and security funding, and the community we would rely on for the needed twenty-five thousand volunteers was dispirited. After going through the financial reports line by line, Mitt warned those involved that the Games would have to be downsized, even joking that it might be necessary to use a backyard grill for the Olympic cauldron. He started by cutting back on expenses, substituting $1-a-slice pizza for the catered food at board meetings and deferring his $280,000 annual salary until the Games were over and financially successful—and then donating it to charity. Then he went to work raising the money that was needed, even going so far as to recruit the first Olympic meat sponsor and first Olympic job search website sponsor.

There wasn't much I could do to help him. From time to time, when I could manage it, I went to Mitt's office, mostly just to help build morale among the staff. It very quickly became a tight-knit group.

Dr. Weiner helped arrange for me to get infused at the University of Utah hospital. While we certainly had halted the progression of the disease, I wasn't getting any better. Once, I remember, we were in an airport waiting room, getting ready to fly back to Boston, and I just had to lie down on the floor. I was overwhelmed. I couldn't stand up without losing my balance, and I didn't have the energy to sit up. As I lay there, I thought, *I don't know if I can do this.* Just getting on an airplane seemed like more than I was capable of. Sometimes I felt like I had a dark cloud over my head all the time. My disease had gone into remission, and while it had been temporarily stopped, that fear of when the other shoe was going to drop was always in the back of my mind. Always.

Yet, as time passed, being in Utah began to make a difference to me. When I was physically able to walk, I set goals for myself. Each day, I was determined to walk just a little farther than I had the previous day. Sometimes I managed only a few more steps, a couple of feet, but even that was a feeling of great victory. I was getting stronger. I could measure my progress.

When Mitt and I started construction on the house in Utah, which seemed in some ways a lifetime before, one of the things I had promised myself I would do was take advantage of the rural setting and start horseback riding again. As a child, it had been my passion, and while other teenage activities had replaced it, it was something I had never forgotten. The thought of being on a horse again was very exciting. In fact, I actually had gone online and found a woman in Park City who was selling a horse. I called and explained to her that I wasn't interested in buying her horse, but that my husband and I were building a house in the area and I wondered if she could recommend someone to give me a few riding lessons.

She gave me a name and phone number, which I wrote down in my daily planner.

That promise had been pretty much put aside with the

onset of MS. But when I finally arrived in Utah, I decided that if, eventually, I lost the use of my legs, I was to take advantage of whatever mobility I had to pursue my passions. I flipped through the planner until I found that number and then picked up the phone to renew that youthful romance.

I grew up in a neighborhood with few homes and lots of space. I was pretty much the only girl in the area, so for survival I learned to play baseball and football; but mostly I played on my own. Like so many other young girls, I fell in love with horses at a young age. I started taking riding lessons when I was eight, and quickly became a barn rat, happily mucking stalls, grooming horses, and learning how to care for them. One of the horses in the barn was a gentle creamy white mare with blue eyes named Sobie, who quickly became my best friend. I would tell her all my secrets, confident she would not share them with anyone. For Christmas 1979, in addition to the usual pile of presents, I found a note telling me, "Go to the mailbox." In the mailbox, I found a second note: "Go to the olive tree." A further series of clues directed me to the garage my father had just built at the bottom of our hill. I hadn't been the least curious about this new project, even after my father put up a white picket fence around it.

I pushed open the garage door and stood there dumbfounded. Rather than a large open area for cars, the structure contained two stalls. And standing right in the middle was Sobie. My Sobie. She was as sweet as any animal possibly could be. For the next few years of my life, I practically lived in that stable. We got another horse, presumably for my brother, but it was really so Sobie wouldn't be alone, and I took care of both of them. I cleaned and filled the troughs, swept the barn, made sure they were fed, and kept them groomed. In the winter, when the pipes froze, I would carry buckets of water down the hill. One freezing cold morning I will never forget, I went down to the stable and broke the ice covering the top of a bucket, reached in to pull out the debris that had settled into it, and instead found myself holding an enormous frozen rat. After that, my father added a metal feed room with raised bins off to the side.

During the school year, I would be in the stable before I left in the morning and go right back there when I got home in the late afternoon, to muck the stalls and feed the horses. I would ride often after school and on weekends. In the summer, that's where I would always be found, and we would go for a ride every day.

Sobie and I were connected emotionally. I learned how to read her moods and communicate with her; I never had to say anything, she would respond to my touch. She must have understood me, too, because somehow she always gave me the response I needed. Eventually, I was so comfortable with her that I didn't really need a saddle or bridle to ride her. I would direct her with my knees.

We had some apple trees not very far from the house, and sometimes, on beautiful summer or fall days, Sobie and I would go there and I would let her roam free; it was a place she loved, too. I would turn around on her, lying on my tummy with my head on her butt, as she walked around eating apples and grass. I felt completely safe; I knew she was going to take care of me. I would watch the drifting clouds, and her gentle movements would rock me. We would wander around for hours like that, listening to nature, enjoying the warmth of the sun and the gentle breeze, feeling totally content. Being with Sobie was my happy place during my childhood.

As I got older my interests changed, and I had less time to care for her. It was the normal cycle of life; I had my life in high school, I had boys to giggle about with my friends, I had all those magical things that occupy the lives of teenage girls. So our rides became less frequent. Then one day I came home from school and she was gone.

My father had sold her. That was him, always practical. He had spoken to me about it, pointing out that I wasn't paying as much attention to the horses and maybe it was time to move on. "You're getting older," he said, reminding me that I was going to leave for college soon. "No, no, no," I'd said, completely dismissing the idea, and then I'd probably gotten on the phone with a friend and forgotten all about his warning. Then Sobie was gone. I knew that it was the right thing to do—I wasn't giving her the attention that any animal needs—but I felt that an important part of my childhood had been yanked away from me. I was so upset. I never saw Sobie again. I hoped she'd found a home with someone with a little girl. I was angry with my father, but that feeling passed over time, and not too long afterward I met Mitt.

I never filled that place in my heart, though. A marriage and raising five children in Boston kept me much too occupied to ride again. I would think about Sobie from time to time, I would tell the boys about her, and I promised myself that sometime I would start riding again. I didn't expect to find that emotional connection that I'd had with that horse, but riding was something that I'd loved deeply. After my diagnosis, and facing an uncertain future, I knew it was time.

Truthfully, I wasn't even certain I would be able to ride. People who haven't ridden have no understanding of how physically difficult it can be to control an incredibly strong animal weighing as much as a thousand pounds. With my balance problems, at times I was having difficulty simply staying upright in a chair, so the concept of sitting in a saddle and commanding an animal made me a little bit nervous. But I believed this might be my last opportunity to find that happy place of my childhood, before my disease made it impossible, so I was determined at least to try.

The first day Mitt and I arrived in Salt Lake, the Olympic Committee held a press conference. It was a major story: the turnaround expert from Boston had come to save the Salt Lake City Olympics. After the conference, I opened my day planner, found the number I had been given, and called a horse trainer named Margo Gogan. I knew nothing about her other than that she was considered to be an excellent teacher, but this was the only name I had.

I introduced myself and told her that my husband and I had just moved into the area and I wanted to start taking lessons. It was obvious she had never heard the name Romney, and I suspected that even if she had, she wouldn't have cared. She very politely told me that she was completely booked and that there was no chance she would be able to add another client to her already filled schedule. Her stalls were full; there just was no room for another horse. She did offer to add me to her waiting list, although she admitted that she didn't know how long it would be until it was my turn.

I wouldn't let her off the phone. The fact that she had no interest at all in training me made me want to train with her even more. I began dropping little hints about why we had come to Utah, mentioning "the Winter Olympics," and eventually I got her attention. "Oh, yes," she finally agreed, "I've heard something on the news about this Mitt Romney guy. That's you?"

As Margo told me later, much later, "I thought Ann Romney was an awfully pushy broad, but I'm pretty pushy, too. The Olympics were very important to all of us living here, and I thought if she and her husband were coming all the way to Utah to help us with this, the least I could do was meet her."

Margo had no idea that this stranger was about to burst into her life. She expected to meet some aggressive woman, give her some information and recommendations about other equestrian centers in the area, shake hands, and send her on her way. I believed I had a limited amount of time to fulfill this promise I'd made to myself, and I intended to spend each minute wisely. So I put on a pair of riding breeches and drove out to meet her. I was going to ride.

What possessed me to put on those jodhpurs I will never know, but I wanted this woman to know I was serious, that I was ready to get started right away. I really wanted this.

The good news was that when I walked into the barn wearing breeches and a little riding hat, she didn't laugh at me.

Margo was tall, about five eight, and wore her blond hair in a casual ponytail, and everything about her exuded calm and confidence. We connected the moment we started talking. I told her the truth about my disease; I wanted her to know what she was getting into. It didn't seem to bother her at all. I pretty much recognized in Margo the same streak of practicality that I have: This is what it is; you can do it or you can't do it. You can spend all day wishing, but you'll get a lot more accomplished with one minute of doing. That first day was incredible. Within a few minutes we had gotten away from horses and were talking about those things in life that really matter. We talked about spiritual things, about family, God, what Mitt and I had been doing in Boston, and how scary it was to have been diagnosed with MS.

Among the things about Margo that immediately appealed to me was her bluntness. She asked a question I supposed a lot of people had wondered about but no one had asked: How did it feel to have something that money couldn't fix or make go away? I wasn't hesitant about answering that, telling her that money had never been the essential aspect of our lives. While Mitt and I appreciated what we had—and boy, did we know how fortunate we were—the things that mattered to us really were those things money couldn't buy: our love for each other, our family, and our church. It just had never been part of our thinking that being wealthy would or should insulate us from life's challenges. And while obviously having money made dealing with the ramifications of the disease simpler, it didn't change who I was. In fact, as I would learn much later, the stages that I was working my way through were common for anyone who has faced a sudden and life-changing challenge, whatever their financial situation. I had gone through the first stage, denial. I had accepted the reality of my situation, and I had set out to make the best of it. I knew there was no cure for MS, but I was determined to fight it as much as I was capable of doing—and the best way to do that was to live the best life possible.

By the time we were finished talking, we were friends, having bonded over our love for horses. It was a friendship that would only grow through the years. For me, one of the hardest aspects of moving to Salt Lake had been leaving Laraine. We spoke on the phone, and she would come out to visit, but I missed having her around on a day-to-day basis. While our friendship with Laraine would endure, and we still often meet in various places for events and celebrations, Margo filled the huge void.

In so many ways we were alike. Like me, Margo had fallen in love with horses when she was a young girl. Watching the equestrian competition in the Olympics when she was ten years old, she noted that the riders held their reins in two hands. "I'm a little girl from out west," she said, "where it's all rodeo and western. I wanted to ride with two reins and I just pestered and pushed until it happened. When I was eleven, I learned to weld and helped my father build a barn. When the barn was finished and ready for horses to be let in, he let me stay home from school. 'You know why I let you miss school for this?' he asked. I shook my head, and he told me, 'Just be still and listen.' I did, and the only sound was the horses munching on the hay. 'Now just smell that smell.' The fresh wood, the fresh shavings, reminded me of Christmas. I never forgot that. That barn became my safe haven, the place I could go and be alone with my horses."

Several members of Margo's family were musicians; an uncle even played with the San Francisco Philharmonic. Margo didn't have that ability, so she decided that "the horse would be how I expressed myself. We groom the arena every day—meaning we'd break up dirt clods and level the earth—and I love to have the first ride in the morning. I make my own designs on the ground." Some mornings I would get there early enough to see her carefully grooming the dirt on her tractor while opera music, usually Andrea Bocelli, blared from the loudspeakers.

I had spent my life in the cities of the Midwest and the East, while she was a westerner who loved open spaces, but I knew we'd found our common ground when she said, "I may not be able to speak to people in their language, but I can speak to any horse anywhere in the world."

At seventeen she started teaching hunters and jumpers, but eventually focused on dressage, and became one of the most respected teachers of that type of riding. Dressage is a really difficult sport. Often called horse ballet, it is a five- or six-minute choreographed performance often set to music in which a horse and rider have to perform a series of both mandatory and optional movements that highlight the grace, beauty, and power of the animal, and its connection to the rider. The rider's objective is to make it look easy, almost as if he or she isn't doing anything but sitting straight up on the horse while out for a comfortable ride. (In fact, the better a rider is, the less it looks like she is doing.) In fact, the rider is controlling every movement of the horse, every change of direction, every change in its gait, with subtle motions such as applying pressure with a leg and shifting weight. The rider isn't even permitted to use voice commands to control the horse. In competitions, as many as seven judges rate each horse and rider against the accepted standards, the way gymnastics is judged, rather than rating them against other competitors.

I had never done dressage, but it seemed perfect for me. There is no jumping, and the horse is always under control, so it cuts down any possible risk—although, at some point, everybody gets thrown. When I first started learning dressage, I asked Margo about how long it would take to become good at it, and she smiled and guessed, "Maybe ten years." It's similar to Mitt trying to perfect his golf swing—it's a sport where you are never going to reach perfection, but the challenge is to continue improving.

Although I was completely honest with Margo about my MS, I insisted she not take it easy with me. I wanted her to train me exactly the way she worked with her other students. "Oh, don't worry about that," she said, a promise she certainly fulfilled. Margo explained that she had some experience working with people with disabilities. Only a few years earlier, she had trained the young son of a friend of hers who was suffering from cerebral palsy. His disability was far more pronounced than mine; he had only limited control over his body. Margo and her friend figured out a way to keep him safely secured in the saddle using Velcro. The horseback riding proved to be a very important aspect of his therapy. In fact, there is a long history of horses being used for therapeutic purposes, especially with children. Horses seem to have an intuitive sense of how to work with people with disabilities. Apparently, as I learned, riding offers physical, emotional, and psychological benefits: For people who can't walk, being on a horse is as close as they can get to having legs that work. They benefit from balancing in the saddle, which stimulates circulation and respiration and tones the same muscle groups as those used in walking. For someone like me, it helps build postural strength. Some research shows that it also affects the central nervous system, helping people harmonize their movements. Yet my motive for starting to ride again wasn't for any type of therapy. I wasn't doing this because of my MS. I wanted to do it in spite of my MS. This was a long-delayed pleasure I had earned.

That first day, Margo and I sat talking for almost an hour. Then she suggested, "Let's see what you can do." I leaped at the chance, quickly pulling on my riding boots— except they no longer fit. The steroid treatments had made my whole body puffy. I felt like one of Cinderella's stepsisters trying to force her foot into the glass slipper. But I managed to get up on a horse that day, and within seconds I understood the derivation of the expression "back in the saddle again." It means regaining a comfort level in the performance of a task. I hadn't ridden in more than three decades, but the feelings came roaring back. As a rider, I did everything wrong: I was bouncing all over the place. I had no strength at all. I was pulling on a rein to hold on, which meant I was pulling on the horse's mouth. That horse and I were completely out of rhythm. To someone like Margo, watching me ride that horse must have been like Leonard Bernstein listening to an elementary school recital. But I loved it.

I took one ride around the small arena—it was only about 150 feet by 75 feet, so tiny—but I learned within a few seconds that dressage is much more physically tiring than it looks. In less than a minute I was exhausted. In dressage, the rider doesn't slump over the saddle, holding on to the horn as he or she would on a trail ride. There is no saddle horn to hold on to, so the rider has to hold her entire core upright while relaxing her arms and legs and trying to absorb the movement of the horse—all while still exerting enough force to control this big animal. Margo once described it as trying to stay on a narrow balance beam that's in motion. By the time I finished that single loop, I was exhausted—exhilarated but exhausted. Just one loop had drained all my energy.

I had to lean over and rest on that old horse's neck. But I couldn't wait to do it again. It wasn't as if the depression that had been surrounding me suddenly lifted and the sun shone brightly, but at least there was a break in the overcast. It would be more than a month before I made a complete circuit of the arena without having to pause to regain my strength. The first time I managed to do it, Margo just nodded her head in approval. Neither of us made a big deal about it, but inside I was thrilled. It was so hard to measure progress in my new life. This was now a milestone.

I rode Margo's training horses for several sessions. Before any real teaching can be done, a rider has to get comfortable on horseback. Beginners in dressage need to ride experienced and tolerant horses that are calm in the arena and willing to work with an inexperienced rider. They are the equine equivalent of a bike with training wheels. Their purpose is to help a rider overcome any fears and apprehension. The next step is for a rider to get her own horse and train with it until the horse and rider are a team. It is one thing to get on a horse and lead it through the mechanics, the programmed movements, but doing it beautifully requires developing a real partnership with the animal. It means getting to know and understand the horse on a very deep level. It means working with the horse in the arena, being with it in the barn, grooming it and caring for it. The horse has to trust its rider completely—but the rider also has to have confidence in the horse. Eventually, the horse and rider will develop their own unique means of communication, and it's different with every horse. When it happens, though, the team goes through its paces in complete harmony. While it's a beautiful thing to watch, it's even better to be part of that special relationship.

It often takes as long as a year for a new rider to be ready to take that step, but I was in a big rush. I didn't know how much longer I'd physically be capable of riding. After only a few weeks Margo was satisfied that I could handle myself on a horse, so it was time to find the right horse for me.

I came into the barn one morning and Margo told me she had the perfect horse for me: a grandson of the great Secretariat. I was instantly impressed. Many people consider Big Red, as Secretariat was affectionately known, the greatest racehorse of all time. I assumed his grandson would reflect the same noble bearing. When Margo led me into the barn and introduced me to Buddy, I guessed he had come from the other side of the family. Although he had the same chestnut coloring for which his grandfather was known, the resemblance stopped there. Secretariat had spent fifteen years in stud and had sired six hundred foals, but few of them had even a small percentage of his great heart and speed. And Buddy clearly was not one of them.

Buddy had been born in Margo's stalls, so she had a great deal of affection for him. He had a good straight back, strong legs, and correctly aligned hooves—but truthfully, he was pretty unspectacular. Well, he certainly wasn't intimidating like his grandpa. Still, he was a beautiful horse in his own way. Margo led him out of his stall. I got on and took a brief ride around the arena. I felt completely comfortable on him. He was a lackluster horse, but then, I was a lackluster rider. We were a perfect match.

After a single lap we left the arena and started up a hill that took us away from the barn. Just Buddy and me. And as we rode up that gradual slope I was overcome with emotion. The previous few months had been an unending whirlwind of life-changing events. As we moved slowly toward the top of the hill, a wave of emotional memories flooded my body. I was fourteen years old again and healthy and free.

We meandered toward a peak that allowed us to over-look the beautiful Heber Valley. Buddy answered every slight tug on the reins. I was on the top of the mountain looking out at the Wasatch Mountains, and for the first time in months I felt strong enough to cry.

In those few minutes, Buddy and I formed our relation-ship. From that moment on, we were completely comfort-able. It was as if I was finally able to take one very deep, very long breath. Tears I had been holding back streamed down my face. When we got back to the barn, Margo looked at me with concern. Was I okay? Was everything all right? Everything's fine, I told her. It was just so beautiful. "I feel like a girl of fourteen again."

After that, I went to the barn every day I was able to, to do whatever I could to help. The equestrian center was like going home for me, and I didn't want to leave. I wanted to groom my horse, I wanted to muck the stall, I wanted to put the blankets on and comb his mane. I was dirty and exhausted, and I wore out very fast, but while I had the energy, it was so much fun for me. I met all the girls at the barn, and we would sit and talk, and when we did, I would hear the echo of my own early years. They were young, inde-pendent, and sassy; they could throw a saddle on a horse, go out into the woods, and cut lumber with their chainsaw, and be back home in time to get a manicure and have their hair done. My world was opening up again.

Mitt was thrilled that I had found something so mean-ingful to me, although he didn't understand it at all. We'd met soon after Sobie was sold, and I had pretty much stopped riding, so while he'd heard all the stories, we had lived our whole life without horses being part of things. Now suddenly the poor guy had to adjust to this whole new world, and truthfully, he was kind of baffled by it. For a time he thought it was just going to be something that excited me temporarily, that I would enjoy it and then something else would attract my attention. So he was surprised, and eventually very pleased, when he accepted the fact that horses were going to be a permanent part of our life. Eventually he began telling people that he wanted to send me to the Betty Ford Clinic for Horse Addiction, but he finally realized that there is no cure for it.

Still, he worried. Riding can be very dangerous. Mitt has reminded me often that the most frequent injuries seen in emergency rooms are motorcycle accidents and horseback riding injuries. Riders do get hurt, they break fingers and hands, and unfortunately sometimes they suffer far more grievous injuries. When I went to Margo's, I already had a bad back and I knew that riding could be very jarring on your spine, so there was at least the possibility that riding would damage my back further. But there was no room for any more fear in my life. I was determined to do this.

Probably no one was more startled to see me on a horse than Laraine. Ann on a horse? In Boston I had never been around horses or even talked about my love for them. Yet when Laraine came to visit, I took her right to the barn to show her Buddy. She must have thought she had stumbled into another world. The Ann Romney she knew had nothing to do with horses. But that other Ann didn't exist anymore. "I just can't get over this," she kept saying. "You are so brave to get on that huge animal!" When she saw the happiness and strength I got from riding, she didn't question it; she just shook her head in amazement and enjoyed it.

When I began riding, I asked Dr. Weiner for his opinion—not his permission. Unless there was some serious risk, I was determined to do it. "How does it make you feel?" he asked. Great, I told him. "Then enjoy it," he said. His philosophy is that there is no universal treatment for MS. Everyone reacts differently. The only restriction he ever suggested to me was that I should be smart and trust my body to tell me when it was time to quit. So if someone with MS wants to eat a certain food, visit a different country, or start horseback riding, as long as it isn't dangerous he will encourage them to do it. And if it seems to help, he'll try to learn something from it that might eventually benefit other patients.

Finding my passion, finding Margo, who first helped me fulfill it, proved to be extraordinarily important for me, both for getting rid of my depression and for learning how to live with this disease. If Dr. Weiner's care was the first piece of this puzzle I had to put together, then finding my passion and pursuing it was another vitally important piece. When people ask me how to recover from life-changing events, I always suggest they find their passion. For me, finding something that brought me this much joy at that point in my life made all the difference. It brought me all the way to a very happy place in my life. It made getting out of bed in the morning exciting to me. The second I got up, I would have breakfast and then tear out of the house to go to the barn. I was so excited to be physically able to get up and go that at times I probably pushed myself harder than I should have, and it took its toll, but as soon as I regained my stamina, I was back at it.

I had so much to learn. As a young girl I'd never had any formal instruction. I'd basically galloped around, trusting Sobie. But Margo taught me the rudimentary skills of dressage; the basic walk, trot, canter; how to post; even how to sit properly on a horse. Buddy, wonderful, patient Buddy, was completely understanding as I fumbled to master those movements. Several of them were especially difficult for me, because my body wouldn't cooperate. At times it got very frustrating. My brain would tell my muscles what to do, and my muscles would not respond. It was very difficult for me, for example, to learn how to keep my right leg down. I'd lost control of the nerves in that leg, and if I didn't focus my attention on it, it would just creep up. Margo was always screaming at me, "Get your right heel down! Get your right heel down!" She knew it was hard for me, so she helped by reminding me, often and loudly. Out of frustration, sometimes I'd shout at it, too. I had to discover strategies to compensate for such problems. For example, I cheated just a little by having my stirrups a little shorter than normal.

Getting thrown off your horse is pretty common in dressage. Everybody who rides eventually hits the dirt, and no one knew how my body would respond to that. Well, we found out about three months after I started riding, when Buddy bucked me off for the first time. Buddy was a good boy, and I felt safe on him, but one afternoon we were outside and I was talking to a vet. I was relaxed, I had a loose rein, my legs weren't even in the stirrups. Buddy's head was down and he was quiet. Suddenly a little dust devil, a whirl-ing, twirling burst of wind, came out of nowhere. It picked up a chair and tossed it. Buddy reacted instantly, bucking and taking off. Without the reins in my hands, and with my feet out of the stirrups, there was nothing I could do. I probably could have held on; his bucking wasn't especially violent. Instead, I decided, *I'll get off now*—and I got ejected. I was about to land on my butt, so I put down my hands to protect myself—and broke fingers on both hands. It hurt, but I was able to get right back up. My body was able to take that blow without suffering any serious consequences.

While we knew the challenges I faced were going to be difficult, we were somewhat surprised that Mitt's task with the Olympics had turned out to be much more com-plex than we envisioned. While there was very little I could do to help him on a daily basis, I did make what came to be an important contribution: I bought him a horse.

Actually, I bought trail horses for both of us. I surprised Mitt with a beautiful Palomino named Trigger. My reason for this was obvious: riding Buddy had proven to be incred-ibly important therapy for me. It was all-consuming. It required such focus that while I was doing it, I forgot com-pletely about my disease. During that time, my mind was in a different place. Then, within an hour afterward, that feel-ing of euphoria would fade and I'd remember I didn't feel so good anymore.

I thought riding might have similar benefits for Mitt. For a brief period of time it would allow him to escape the overwhelming stress, to get away from the seemingly end-less problems he had to deal with every day. Mitt knew how to ride. Earlier in his life he had worked on a ranch. While, as far as the boys were concerned, he had been a cowboy riding the range, he'd actually spent most of the time driving a tractor in a cornfield. But he had also rounded up cattle, set posts, and strung barbed wire, so he was comfortable on a western-style horse.

At least that's what I believed. But one of the first times he had to mount his horse, on the side of a mountain, he'd forgotten to tighten the girth. As he began to mount, the horse lowered its neck to chew some grass and Mitt just kept going—right over the horse's neck.

I soon discovered that Mitt really wasn't very knowledgeable about horses. Almost every weekend from May to October, we would saddle our horses and ride up into the mountains. We'd start the morning with a big breakfast at Chick's Café, a diner in Heber City, and then go out into the pasture to get our horses. Time had frozen in Heber City back in the 1950s, so it was like riding back in time. One Saturday, I was getting our saddles and I told Mitt to go into the pasture, get his horse, and bring it back. He returned a few minutes later, holding the reins of a beautiful horse. "Well, that's certainly a nice horse, Mitt," I told him, "but it's not yours." The horse was vaguely the same color as Mitt's horse, and it also had four legs and a tail, so Mitt brought it back.

Mitt loved these Saturdays. It was the first time— literally the first time—we could just be together without our children. It was such a new experience for us, not having to go from children's activity to children's activity. We had spent thirty years focusing on our kids, and suddenly it was just the two of us again. We tried to spend as much time together as possible; we both saw that cloud hanging over my future and wanted to grab every single moment of life while I still had the physical capability. But horse riding also had the effect on him that I had hoped: it became an escape for him, too. He would throw his leg over the saddle, settle in, and start singing. He actually has a melodious voice, but what he lacked in range he more than made up in volume. He was instantly able to put aside his cares and live entirely in the moment.

Usually we went by ourselves, although many times Kem Gardner would join us. We would pack a lunch and ride into the mountains, leaving all our concerns below. We'd ride around the huge trees and across streams. We'd see the variety of forest animals, from beavers to moose, as we moved away from the realities of our daily life into the peace of nature. Eventually we'd reach a beautiful grassy meadow, where we'd tether our horses, spread a blanket, and picnic on the mountainside. We'd sit there quietly, in no hurry to complete the next task, return the last phone call, make the next appointment, or schedule another meeting. It was as if we were refueling. Through all the difficult moments, neither one of us ever forgot for a moment how truly lucky we were, and we often offered a prayer of gratitude in that meadow. By the time we started down the mountain again, we'd feel ready for whatever was awaiting down there.

Taking up riding had made a fundamental difference in my life. Instead of wishing that I would die quickly rather than be devoured piece by piece, as I had been thinking only a few months earlier, it helped me learn to live with my disease. I was beginning to figure out the warning signs for when I was about to collapse and develop strategies for dealing with them. I had gotten at least a little comfortable being able to tell people I was done, while not feeling bad about it. And more and more I was appreciative of all the things that I was able to do, rather than being angry about what I could no longer do.

And I was learning dressage. That was a great challenge. I spent a lot of hours bouncing around in the saddle before I began to make progress. Riding had done so much for me. It helped me feel better physically, it helped lift my depression, it allowed me at least briefly to forget all about my MS, it allowed me to meet an entirely new group of friends and a sweet animal who put up with my failings, and most of all, it gave me Margo. Margo's joy resonated throughout the barn and was reflected in all the people who worked there. While she would push me past my comfort zone as far as she could, encouraging me to go around one more time, just one more time, there were days when I didn't have enough energy to ride for more than a few minutes. When that happened we'd just sit and talk, often discussing dressage techniques and strategies, but just as often talking about our problems. With Margo, everything is directed toward some wonderful point in the future. Later I would tell people that nobody would need a therapist if they had a Margo in their life.

Mitt and I had settled nicely in Salt Lake City. For me, to my surprise and pleasure, it had turned out to be a beginning rather than an end.

Four

IT WAS JUST SO HARD for me to accept the fact that there was no cure for MS. Throughout my life I had seen medical science making one incredible breakthrough after another. I was just a little girl when polio was eliminated. Surgeons had learned how to transplant organs and restore hearing to the deaf. Scientists had greatly reduced the number of deaths from heart disease and cancer. Orthopedic surgeons were implanting artificial joints to restore lost mobility. It seemed that every day I was reading about some kind of new miracle cure or treatment or breakthrough— so it was hard for me to understand why researchers had made such little progress in discovering the causes, effective treatment methods, or potential cures for MS, ALS, Parkinson's disease, Alzheimer's disease, brain tumors, or any of the whole range of neurologic diseases. (Researchers actually knew more about MS than they did about ALS or Alzheimer's disease.)

At least with MS they understood what happened in the brain to cause the symptoms, but they didn't know why it started, how it progressed, why each case was so different, how to prevent it or stop it, how to cure it, or how to repair a damaged brain. Dr. Weiner had proven that, in some cases, steroids could slow down the progression of the disease and even alleviate some of the symptoms, but even he didn't understand why they worked only for certain patients. If I needed a new heart, they could give me one. If I needed new knees, that was easy. It would take only a couple of hours to restore my vision to near its original acuity. But there was no cure for my disease.

Disorders of the brain remain one of the great medical mysteries. People have been trying for centuries to find something, anything, that might make a difference. Between 5000 and 3000 BC, Indian physicians were treating a disease remarkably similar to Parkinson's with the root of *Withania somnifera* (also known as Indian ginseng), the seed of *Mucuna pruriens* (Bak), the root of *Sida cordifolia* (country mallow), and the fruit of *Hyoscyamus reticulatus* (henband). In the seventh century BC, the physician and mathematician Pythagoras described dementia as the last of the six phases of life, when "mortal existence closes . . . where the mind is reduced to the imbecility of the first epoch of infancy."

Physicians in almost every civilization have used potions, herbs, and incantations to treat these diseases. In the sixteenth century, Renaissance alchemists were prescribing gold preparations for a range of neurologic and psychiatric disorders. By the eighteenth century, quacks were marketing an array of completely useless elixirs and bizarre treatments to desperate people willing to pay for them. Even into the twentieth century, supposedly enlightened scientists were conducting lobotomies, literally cutting out pieces of the brain, in the belief that they might cut out the diseased area without causing permanent neurologic damage.

Before I was diagnosed and learned that there was no cure, it was a lot easier for me to shake my head in disbelief that people would turn to unusual treatments. But after my diagnosis, when a friend of a friend, a very intelligent and rational woman, suggested I investigate alternative medicine, I listened to her. The reason is pretty obvious: Why not? What did I have to lose by trying different treatments? Many of the people I'd spoken with told me about various alternative treatments that had worked for them. They pointed out that there was no scientific evidence to support a specific treatment, so they couldn't tell me *why* it had worked, only that *it had worked*. I remember talking to Dr. Weiner about this, and he was surprisingly open to it. "The brain is a very powerful force in terms of our health," he told me. "For example, I always teach doctors that it's vitally important to leave every patient with hope. I don't want them to lie, but I want them to create hope. A positive attitude can be very important, wherever it comes from. We don't know what it does precisely, but we do know it can make a difference."

That phrase, alternative medicine, covers a lot of territory. In recent years it has come to include many different potential treatments outside science-based Western medicine. For example, it includes holistic medicine, which treats the whole person rather than the specific disease. It's one of the oldest forms of therapy. In the fourth century BC, Socrates warned that treating one part of the body was not sufficient. Another form of medicine is the traditional Hindu practice of ayurveda, a plant-based pseudoscientific approach. The list of potential treatments is long. People have found value in meditation, homeopathy, massage and spinal manipulation, and certainly acupuncture, yoga, diet, supplements, aromatherapy, biofeedback, herbs, and spices.

Before that first long phone call with this wonderful friend of a friend, for example, I had never heard of craniosacral therapy, developed in the 1970s. It sounds a little strange. Essentially a practitioner lightly touches your skull, face, spine, and pelvis, which supposedly causes spinal fluid to move around until it is in balance. At one time, I probably would have dismissed it without much thought, but when this woman told me that it had made a big difference in her life, I paid attention. While Dr. Weiner's treatments appeared to have stopped the progression of the disease, at least temporarily, I was still very weak and got tired quickly. And the infusions always left me feeling awful. Resuming riding had been a tremendous boost for my spirit, and had helped lift my depression, but it hadn't had much of an impact on my symptoms. I was still too tired too often.

When I got to Salt Lake City, the idea of trying alternative medicine had drifted to the back of my mind. Then my back went out, and a friend suggested I go to a reflexologist for help. My initial reaction was humor: my back hurts; why would you press on my feet? I had been suffering from back pain for ten years. I had first herniated a disc while water skiing, and had had many episodes in the years since. I would go through the usual course of taking pain medication, lying on my back, and doing physical therapy. As anyone who has a herniated disc knows, it hurts, and for days after, I would be so crippled by the pain that I couldn't walk on my own. Barbara, a friend of mine, told me, "I got someone you should see. There's a guy I go to when my back goes out. It really helps. He's a reflexologist."

I didn't have the slightest idea what a reflexologist did, or where you went to find one, but my world had changed so completely in the past few months that I was instantly and entirely open to the idea. If she had told me that standing on my head and singing "The Battle Hymn of the Republic" would alleviate my back pain, I would have done that, too. I was far beyond being judgmental about things I didn't understand. Actually, I doubted reflexology would help, but I knew for certain I had nothing to lose.

Reflexology is a distant cousin to acupuncture. As Barbara explained to me, depending on where the pain is, the reflexologist applied pressure with his thumbs on specific places on the bottom of your feet supposedly to stimulate the nerves that run through the source of the pain and increase blood flow to that area. There is absolutely no scientific evidence that it works, except this woman sitting next to me told me it had significantly reduced her back pain. It certainly sounded like hocus-pocus to me, but I wrote down the phone number.

A man with a heavy German accent answered the phone,

but I could hear enthusiasm in his voice. I told him I was having back problems. I didn't say a word about my MS. I didn't feel there was any need to complicate the situation. "Yah," he would see me, he said, and informed me that a session with him would cost ten dollars.

His name was Fritz Blietschau and he lived with his wife in a tiny bungalow home on Fillmore Street. When I arrived, he welcomed me and invited me in. He was an elderly man, in his late seventies, about five foot eight, with silver hair, a confident smile, and sparkling eyes. A stroke had left him weaker on one side, so he walked with a slight limp. His hands, I noticed, seemed a little gnarled, and his thumbs were unnaturally curved. There were two folding chairs opened and facing each other in the small bedroom where I would have my treatment. *Well, this certainly is crazy*, I thought. I'd gone from being treated by some of the finest doctors working in the most sophisticated medical facilities in the world to sitting on a folding chair in a tiny house in Salt Lake City facing an old man about to manipulate my feet. *If this were a movie, I wouldn't believe it for a second*, I thought. *Okay, this is a little nuts, but he seems like a sweet man and he* is *trying to help. Well, I'm already here*, I thought. *I might as well give this a shot. At least I'll get a nice foot massage out of it.* I smiled nervously and sat down.

He gently took my foot in his hands and began pressing his thumbs into it. His thumbs were as strong as iron, and pain instantly rocketed through my body. He smiled sweetly at me, but did not ask how it felt: It felt like a vise squeezing my foot. It was near agony. I couldn't believe this sweet elderly man was so strong. Each time he pressed into my foot, I thought it had to be the most painful thing I'd ever endured—until he moved to the next spot. Then I wished he would go back to the last spot, because that was less painful. As he worked, he explained what he was doing; he was stimulating the nerves, he said, which was why it hurt so much. I really couldn't pay too much attention to what he was saying; I was busy holding on to the edge of the chair while grimacing in pain. After about forty-five minutes, he put my foot down on the floor and said, "Better."

Of course it felt better. He had stopped pressing his thumbs into my foot.

I was so happy to be done with that. *Maybe this was a little nuts*, I kept thinking. At least I had tried it. I suspected this first foray into the world of alternative medicine would also be my last. But when I got up I felt something completely unexpected: nothing. The pain in my back had been greatly reduced. I was standing up straight, which I hadn't been able to manage without pain in several weeks. *Well, this is interesting*, I thought. *This actually helped me.*

"You need to come back," he said. "One treatment is going to help you only a little bit. I can fix it good."

Well, I knew it was worth the ten dollars. There was something so warm about him, so compassionate—plus the reality was that I actually felt better. I agreed to come back. Having gone through it once, I figured, it couldn't possibly be so painful the next time. Later that night, when Mitt asked me about it, I described Fritz to him and admitted that this unusual treatment had helped my back—and as I was explaining the treatment to him, I realized something far more exciting. My exhaustion had been lifted for a brief moment. I also had a strong reaction to the treatment, and was sick. As I look back, I know that toxins were being released. I couldn't ignore the fact that something had happened. Let's see how I feel after my next treatment, I told Mitt.

I felt much more comfortable with Fritz the second time. It took only a few minutes for me to realize I had been wrong about one thing: I'd thought this treatment wasn't going to hurt as much the second time. Yet the pain was intense. It hurt so much that I started sweating.

"Let me tell you something," Fritz said. "I have feeling in my hands. I get feedback from what I feel. You're not good, you're all blocked up." He started going through a list of organs that weren't working right: my adrenal glands weren't working, my liver wasn't functioning correctly, and my kidneys were weak. "They're all sluggish." He looked up at me and asked, "You're very sick, aren't you?"

"I am," I said.

He nodded. "Yah, I treated another woman like you. And she had MS. These things I'm feeling, it feels like that. Do you have MS?"

"I do, yes," I admitted. I was incredulous. I could not believe he had figured it out by touching my feet!

Normally when people learned I had this chronic disease they looked at me with some combination of fear and uncomfortable pity. But not Fritz. He smiled with satisfaction that he'd figured it out. "I knew it was something serious," he said. And then, looking directly at me, he said, "I can help you."

If someone had been telling me this story, I would have found it difficult to believe, but that is just the way it happened. More than that, when he told me he could help me, I believed him. I know it sounds preposterous, but I believed him. "But I have to see you much more. Three times a week, maybe two hours. We can do good."

What's the harm, I thought. I have nothing to lose by trying it.

"It's going to be a little painful, too," he warned. "We have a lot of work to do."

No kidding, I thought. We raised his fee for the two hours to twenty dollars. At first he refused to take it, but I insisted. Just about the only way I could get him to take it was to threaten not to come anymore if he didn't.

I started seeing Fritz at least three times a week. He was right about his treatments being painful; at first my feet were black and blue. And while the pain never completely disappeared, as I got a little stronger it was greatly reduced.

Fritz was a truly lovely human being. Within a few days I began to think of him as my oompa, my German grandfather. Having my feet crunched continued to be excruciatingly painful, but I always looked forward to our sessions. And gradually he began to include other types of therapy. I learned later that he had started studying MS, speaking to other practitioners of alternate medicine, trying to figure out other treatments that might help me. We did breathing exercises. I know now that this is therapeutic.

Fritz had thrown me a lifeline, and I was holding on tight. "Take a deep breath in through your nose, hold the breath, then a deep breath out through your mouth. Repeat five times." We also did very simple yoga poses. He would sit in his chair like a drill sergeant and direct me: "Stand on one foot. Get your foot into a tree position." Then on to the next exercises. "Spin in one direction five times." I couldn't do any of them. Spin? I could barely go around once slowly without losing my balance. If I moved too fast or tried to do too much I would lose my balance completely. But when I regained it, he would repeat his direction. "Good. Now do it again. Three times."

We worked very hard, and it was so good for me. Within a short period, I could stand on one leg, at least briefly. I could get into the tree position and I could turn around two times, then three times, four, five, six times. I could see that I was making progress. Eventually I could turn ten times without losing my balance. There wasn't a lot of medical logic to some of it, and some of it seemed silly—except for the fact that I started feeling better. Whatever we were doing, it was having a positive effect.

It was because of him, I felt certain, that my day began expanding. My days were simple, structured, and limited. I'd get up early, spend time with Margo and the girls at the equestrian center, get a reflexology treatment, and collapse in exhaustion. The rest of the day was a series of small bits and pieces, in which I was able to accomplish very little. Sometimes I would go for a walk, trying to push myself just a little farther than I had the last time. But sometimes it was hard for me to gather enough energy to walk at all. My world had shrunk to that. But after working with Fritz, I could feel the difference. I was making measureable progress, taking small steps, yes—but at least I was moving forward.

After several months I made a big decision. While the cortisone had stopped most of the numbness, it had not made me feel better. It continued to make me feel terrible. And I was getting really tired of being really tired all the time. I felt that the steroids had done their job and now that Fritz was working with me I had something else to hang on to that was safe. So I decided to try to wean myself off the steroids.

I called Dr. Weiner and told him what I wanted to do. If he had advised me against it, I'm not sure what I would have done. But he didn't. He actually was thrilled for me that I felt well enough to do this. "The important thing is we know it works, Ann," he told me. "That isn't always true for everyone. But we've got a weapon to fight this thing. If you start going backward again, we know what to do."

So I jumped in full throttle with my wonderful Fritz. I had gone into this world thinking it was totally crackers, but I had gotten so desperate I was willing to try anything. But when it worked, I became totally curious. I wanted to know so much more about reflexology, about all the different forms of alternative medicine. Fritz was knowledgeable about that whole unusual world.

"When you came in for the first time," he told me in his thick accent, "your aura was practically black."

I stopped him. "My what?" I had no idea what an aura was. I had to ask him several times to repeat the word, and when I still didn't understand him, I asked him to spell it. Even then, I had no idea what he was talking about.

"From one shoulder to the other there's a light all around you that some people can see," he explained. "It's a projection of your electrical energy. The darker it is, the less energy you have. And when you came in, yours was black, which is how I knew you were so sick." He told me about something called Kirlian photography, a method that supposedly captures an aura on film.

When I asked him if he could teach me to see auras, he shrugged. "I don't know. I can't tell you how I do it myself. I just see it."

I've tried to learn, but honestly without any success.

Yes, I do know how crazy some of this sounds. But I don't care. This is the story of how my life was saved, and changed. And my Oompa Fritz was in the middle of making it happen. After a while I stopped questioning any of it. I accepted it and appreciated it.

From time to time, Fritz would tell me he was noticing a slight change in the color of my aura. "It's a little bit gray," or "It's lighter," or after several months of our being together, "I saw a spot of blue." One little spot of blue. And without fail, his comments always would reflect how I was feeling.

We would have long, fascinating conversations as we worked. His grandfather, he told me, had been in charge of the stables for some well-known baron, and Fritz had inherited his love of horses from him. After the war, he escaped from East Germany and came to Salt Lake City because he was a member of the Mormon Church. At some point he had been in China, where he had learned reflexology. We became so close that he began referring to me as his sweet little granddaughter. Eventually he told me that his mission was to cure me of my disease before he died. I would make a joke out of that, but he was serious. He intended to cure me.

There certainly was very little financial gain in it for him. There was no value I could put on how much he was doing for me, but he would never let me pay any more than twenty dollars a session. I offered, I pleaded with him to take more, but he absolutely refused. His ethics were beyond reproach: He expected to be paid for the work that he did and nothing more. At a time when a nice spa visit might have cost one hundred dollars or more, he wouldn't even consider charging more. He knew he had a gift, and his great satisfaction was sharing it.

Coincidently, our middle son, Josh, moved into a house only a few blocks from Fritz and his wife. On occasion he would meet me at Fritz's house and sit with us while Fritz did his work. Initially, like everyone else in my family, Josh was quite skeptical about reflexology. The only type of holistic healing he knew anything about was acupuncture. For him, modern medicine took place in big, brightly lit hospitals. How could an aging man with gnarled fingers accomplish more than the best doctors in the world? I explained it to him as best I could: In holistic medicine, practitioners treat the whole body. If someone has cancer, or even MS, they shouldn't go to a reflexologist expecting to be cured. That's not what it is. It doesn't replace Western medicine; it can be used in addition to science-based treatments. After chemotherapy or, as in my treatment, steroid infusions, it can help you feel better. It'll provide energy. Josh remained skeptical. In fact, all my boys did, but as long as I believed I was getting something out of it, they were willing to humor me. *That's just Mom.* Although, as Josh later admitted, he was pretty surprised when he saw that I had more energy and was able to do certain things I hadn't been able to do before being treated by Fritz.

Finally, Josh became very curious. I practically dared him, "Go and get a treatment and see what you think." So he went to Fritz for a session, more to learn about reflexology than for treatment. Just as I had several months earlier, Josh sat down in the chair expecting to get a hard but relaxing foot massage. I can still see him holding on to the sides of the chair with both hands, his teeth gritted, his knuckles turning white, beads of sweat forming on his forehead as Fritz smiled and dug into his foot. When he started complaining, Fritz told him, "I'll go a little easier, but your mother never complains about it."

Eventually Fritz decided that he would teach Josh the basic principles. When I'm gone, he told him, your mother is going to need some tune-up, and I'll teach you how to do it. Josh became a good student, and eventually began to believe that these treatments released pent-up or blocked energy in the body. Fritz taught him how the different points on your foot related to other parts of your body, and how to break the blockages there. I didn't know it at the time, but Fritz told Josh that he didn't expect to live that much longer and he was worried about what I would do after his death. He wanted Josh to know enough to be able to continue my reflexology therapy.

Sometimes at night, when I was very tired, I would ask Josh for a treatment. He would pull up a chair near the couch and practice what he had learned. While treatments with Fritz would last an hour or more, after fifteen or twenty minutes Josh's hands would start to cramp.

While Josh felt that giving his mother a treatment was a little bit awkward, he knew there were real benefits to it, and that was far more important to him. Admittedly, the concept of an adult man treating his mother by pressing points on her feet is odd.

Mitt was usually sitting there with us, and slowly Josh lured him in. While Mitt continued to believe that reflexology was, in his own words, "a bunch of hoo-ha," his curiosity eventually trumped his intellect. Of course he didn't understand any more than I did why it was working, but he had to admit that it *was* working. He could see the difference standing right in front of him. Eventually he began to ask Josh to show him what he was doing, where to press his thumbs and for how long and how hard, and after he learned, he would work on my feet sometimes, too. After all our years together, most of the time I had a very good idea what he was thinking. But as he sat there pressing his thumbs into my feet, I decided that this time it would be better not to know.

Eventually, though, Mitt did something I never would have anticipated. He made an appointment to see Fritz himself. He had a terrible sciatica attack; he was practically doubled over in pain. I told him, "Go in and see him. It'll either help or it won't."

He was stubborn. "It may work for you," he said. "But it's not going help me." He was pretty sure about that—right up until the time he walked out of Fritz's house standing up straight.

Fritz got the biggest kick out of that. He loved telling people, "You should have seen Mitt come hobbling up. He couldn't even stand up right. He leaves straight as an arrow, off he walks!"

After that Mitt had to find out why it worked so well. That's him: he needs to know. I remember listening to him as he tried to explain it to someone: "These nerves are all connected. If you touch this point in your foot, it's connected to this point in your back or your liver or your kidneys or your different glands." Mitt isn't satisfied until he understands the logic of a process.

I eventually became dependent on Fritz's treatments. Thanks to him and Margo and Dr. Weiner, and the continued support of my family, my health was improving. I used to imagine that I was dragging my bag of rocks up a steep incline. It was difficult and it was slow, but I was making progress. After more than a year of paying just twenty dollars a session, I wanted to find a way to show my appreciation to Fritz, but he made it so difficult. He insisted that he and his wife had what they needed, and he wouldn't take anything else. During our conversations, though, I found out that he had wanted to go back to Germany for a final visit. I decided that was the one thing I could do for him. "This is the deal, Fritz," I told him. "You know you're getting older, you want to see your family, so this is my gift to you: I'm sending you and your wife to Germany." When he started to protest, I stopped him. "You'll really hurt my feelings if you refuse my gift. You've been giving me a gift all this time, and I haven't refused you. You don't have any choice."

With a little persistence I finally turned his no, no, no's into a "yah." He "vould" go, he agreed, but only for me. I was so pleased—until the reality sank in that my Fritz was going away for six weeks. *Uh-oh*, I thought, *what have I done? What am I going to do without him?* That's when Josh offered to step in; and while Fritz was gone, Josh and I met regularly. While he certainly didn't have the knowledge or experience Fritz had, he did a fine job as a substitute—and I didn't have to pay him the twenty dollars.

Mitt and I had come to Salt Lake City three years before the Olympics. The Games were a mess, and I was a mess. Now, with only months to go, so much had changed. The Games were on track, the world would soon be arriving, and I was loving life. I was regaining my strength. My mornings were spent with Margo and the horses, my afternoons with my wonderful Fritz. And then Fritz had a heart attack. I knew he was dying. It was just terrible. Between taking care of me, working with Josh, and getting to know Mitt, he had become an important part of our family. We were all devastated.

I went to see him in the hospital. I was holding his hand, his grip was still strong, and I couldn't stop crying. He realized he was dying and he was at peace with it. I wasn't. I needed him. I kept telling him he had to get better, that

I didn't know what I would do without him. "You can't go," I cried. "You can't go. I can't do this without you." I reminded him that he had promised he would cure me. I wasn't cured, so he couldn't go. It wasn't fair.

"You'll be okay, Ann," he told me. We both knew he was dying and he was trying to comfort me. "I've gotten you ninety percent of the way there."

"I know, but that's not one hundred percent, Fritz."

He tried to smile. "You're on the path," he told me. "You'll be good. You've learned what you have to do to be well. You have to keep riding. Then you find someone else to get you the rest of the way."

"Don't say that," I told him. "I don't know if I can do this without you."

"Of course you can."

He died three days later. I missed him almost as much as I had missed my parents. I had lost my oompa. When I'd met him my body was in shambles and I could barely stand on my feet for any length of time. After working with him for over two and a half years, I wasn't cured, but I was leading a real life once again. That was his legacy to me.

When I finally accepted the fact that Fritz was gone, I started seeing a wonderful Chinese acupuncturist in Park City. He wasn't Fritz—no one was ever going to be Fritz—but I had learned that I had to keep doing this to maintain my energy; otherwise the fatigue would overwhelm me. I have never found another Fritz, but after we moved back to Boston I found a reflexologist. I don't see her regularly anymore, but when my body got run down and I started getting those signals I know so well, I'd visit the reflexologist or an acupuncturist for, as Fritz would call it, a little tune-up.

It would be impossible to overestimate the importance of having Margo and Fritz, Laraine and my family, in my life at that time. Nobody can—or should have to—get through a life-altering transition without the help of family and friends. Each of these people filled an important space in my life. But there was one other person who came into my life at that time who made a huge difference.

Margo's equestrian center had become my refuge. I had a whole life there. In addition to riding, I worked with the horses as much as my health allowed. I was involved in every aspect of their care, even clipping them myself. During the winter, horses grow heavy coats to help protect them from the cold. You can't really ride them like that, because they sweat a lot, and if their coats get wet, they don't dry easily and the horse will get sick. To prevent this from happening, the coat has to be clipped. It's done with shears, and it's hard to do and takes a long time. A lot of people hire groomers to do it; I wanted to do it myself. A good groomer will do it evenly, and the horse will look beautiful. I wasn't very good at it. Mine ended up looking like a mess, but I didn't care. I was having the time of my life being in the barn with the girls, working as opera music played in the background. Other people thought of it as work, but for me it was the most fun in the world. The concept that grooming horses was therapy had never occurred to me, but I loved being in the barn clipping away.

In fact, I spent so much time there that at one point Josh gave Mitt a rubber horse mask, telling him, "Maybe Mom will pay as much attention to you as she does to the horses."

It was at that barn that I met the other person who filled an important need, Jan Ebeling. Jan was one of the leading dressage riders and teachers in the country. In addition to operating a well-known center in Moorpark, California, he traveled around the country holding two- and three-day clinics. He would see students at Margo's center about once a month or once every six weeks. Like Fritz, Jan had immigrated to the United States from Germany. In 1998 he became an American citizen and that same year represented this country in international competition for the first time. I was very nervous about meeting him. But Margo insisted he could help me reach the next level in dressage. There are ten levels in dressage, leading up to the Grand Prix. I was at the basic training level. Even getting to the next level was a challenge for me.

He watched as I rode around the arena. I did the very best I could, and Margo was supportive. But I learned almost immediately that the only thing that Fritz and Jan had in common was their German background. While Fritz was supportive and consoling, Jan was a taskmaster. While Fritz (and Margo) would pull you to get better, Jan would push you. And he pushed hard.

What I did not know, of course, was that Margo had told him about my condition, and while to me he seemed very tough, he knew exactly what he was doing and he was watching carefully for signs of fatigue. In fact, without my being aware of it, he tailored our forty-five-minute sessions to fit my capabilities. But there were always convenient breaks in each lesson.

At that moment, he was exactly the type of teacher, and person, I needed. I had reached the point in which I had to take the next step. For the previous year, everything I'd done had been based on the status of my MS. People like Margo had given me leeway. My performance had been acceptable—for someone suffering from MS. Mitt always understood completely when I couldn't attend an Olympic function. As much as I did not want to be defined by my disease, there was no escaping it—or at least until I met Jan. I don't believe at that point Jan had ever worked with anyone with a disability, so there was very little flexibility in his teaching. When we were working, he held me to the same standards as his other students. If I had to sum it up, I would say that at the beginning, Margo provided as much therapy as training, while Jan focused on the training. In some ways he reminded me of the character Tom Hanks plays in *A League of Their Own*, as I could almost see him shaking his head and telling me, "There's no crying in dressage!"

Jan was not interested in excuses; he was interested only in performance. As he will always remind his students, no matter how well you do, there is always room for improvement. That was perfect for my personality. I'm one of those people who just won't quit until I'm almost dead. A year earlier we probably couldn't have worked together; physically I wasn't capable of giving just a little more, doing one more circuit of the arena, or sitting up a little taller. But all the work I had been doing with Margo and Fritz was paying off. I was getting stronger. Margo would push me to the edge of my comfort zone, but Jan pushed me right through my fatigue barrier. The two of them formed the perfect team for me.

When I first started training with Jan it took us some time to understand each other. There were some difficult moments. But eventually he understood how hard I was working, and while he never stopped pushing me—"do it again, do it right this time"—he accepted the fact that when I put up my hand and said "uncle," I really did have nothing left. I have been working with Jan for years now, and as with Fritz and Margo, he and his wife, Amy, and their son, Ben, have become extended members of my family. So many vistas have been opened up to me since I started on a new path with my disease—the blessings are too many to count, but I will count them as part of the beautiful picture of my new life.

Dressage is beautiful to watch, even if you don't understand the scoring system, but it is a highly competitive sport. And after working at it diligently, sometimes riding twice a day, after watching endless videos and practicing moves and doing exercises and reading books, after almost two years living in Utah, I wanted to compete. When I told Fritz this, he was completely supportive. I was realistic: I didn't even think about the possibility of winning. Just being able to compete was winning for me.

There is a disabled category in dressage. It is recognition of the fact that, like me, many people with handicaps have discovered the healing nature of riding. I still had only limited control over the right side of my body, and some of our friends suggested I start by riding in that category. Get your feet wet, they suggested. I knew they meant well; they were worried about me failing. But in my mind what I heard was *accept your disability*. I refused to do that. I wanted to measure myself against a wider group of competitors.

There are thousands of competitions for riders on every level held across America each year. An event is almost a pageant. It's held in a beautifully groomed arena with flowers set around the perimeter. Competitors wear traditional riding clothes, the horses are carefully braided. To a new competitor, especially someone like me, who too often focused on my inadequacies rather than my strengths, it can be overwhelming. And knowing that my body was not adjusting well to stress made it even more difficult. I was trying very hard not to get stressed out worrying about becoming stressed out.

The first big competition for me was in Santa Fe. While Jan taught skills, he emphasized the mental aspect of riding, pointing out that your mind controls your movements. The fact that his lessons were also applicable to my disease did not escape me. "Negative thinking is a pattern you can fall into," he would often remind me, "especially when something dramatic happens. If you're focusing on something bad that happened, your thinking can spiral out of control." About an hour before a test or a performance, Jan would visualize his entire ride in real time, breathing as if he were on the horse.

I was too nervous, and too inexperienced, to do anything close to that. I'd been through my routine countless times in training, and had shown only in small shows. While I was warming up, I was so nervous that my mouth went dry and I started breathing irregularly. I remembered one of the basic tenets of riding that Margo had taught me: "The horse mirrors the rider." I knew that if my horse realized how nervous I was, we would be in for a rough ride. I went through my last-minute mental checklist, reminding myself that I had to compensate for the weakness in my right side. Then one of the judges rang the bell, the signal for me to begin.

The way judges score, Margo told me, was to start with an image of what a perfect ten would look like, and then count off the points as the rider failed to perform to that level. I made it easy for them. I got through my entire routine without embarrassing myself, or Margo or Jan, but I made endless errors. I didn't control my horse enough to keep it moving straight, my seat was unsteady, and the elements of my performance were sloppy. I would have judged myself terribly.

The judges were a little kinder. Just a little. But honestly, I wasn't disappointed. Less than two years after arriving in Salt Lake with my MS at its peak, and having not been on a horse in several decades, I was competing without embarrassing myself or making anyone feel sorry for me. Rather than being dispirited at not-so-good marks, I was elated. Failure had never felt more like success. I couldn't wait to get back to work to prepare myself for my next competition. I joyfully showed my scorecard to Margo and Jan and asked, "What did I do wrong?"

Fortunately, neither of them suggested, "Taking up the sport." Instead they picked the area that needed the most improvement and we began working on it.

As the opening of the Winter Olympics got closer I was able to measure my progress in other ways. One of them was a gift to me from Mitt. When we'd arrived in Salt Lake, I hadn't been able to walk all the way up the hill on Main Street. Now I was able to walk up and even down again if I had to. Mitt, meanwhile, had fought the countless battles necessary for Salt Lake to host the Winter Olympics successfully. He had worked more than full-time for almost two years. Once, we went thirteen consecutive days without really seeing each other, even though we were sharing the same bed: Because of my lack of stamina, I already would be asleep when he got home at the end of the day, and I would still be asleep the following morning when he left to get back to the office. His efforts had more than paid off: the funds had been raised, the venues were completed on time, the infrastructure was in place, the volunteers were assigned, event tickets were sold, there was a large surplus in the bank, and there was even snow on the mountains. Mitt was so deeply involved in every aspect of the Games that when there was a tremendous traffic backup on the first day of skiing, he got into the middle of the street and began directing traffic around the bottleneck.

Part of the planning included preparations for the Winter Olympics Torch Relay, a tradition that began exactly fifty years earlier, in Oslo, Norway. This relay carries the torch from Olympia, Greece, to the site of the games, where the torch for that Olympics is lit. A variety of people are honored by carrying the torch a short distance. In the United States 12,012 people would be selected to carry the torch 13,500 miles, passing through 46 different states. For the Salt Lake City Games the theme of the relay was "Inspire," and Americans were encouraged to nominate people who had inspired them for this honor. The Salt Lake Olympic Committee was permitted to select 3,500 people—and received more than 50,000 nominations. Many people on the committee felt that Mitt should carry the torch, as his work had ensured the Games would be a success. Mitt refused, and instead nominated me. It was a wonderful gesture, but initially I was a little embarrassed by it. I read many of the hundred-word essays nominating people and was really touched by them. These were average Americans, the kind of people who are never in the headlines, but who spend their time helping others by their work or the example they set. These were teachers and doctors, blind students who tutored others, firefighters who risked their lives to save others, people in wheelchairs living full and productive lives. In our celebrity-based culture, it was gratifying to see these people receive even a little bit of the recognition and appreciation they had earned. And boy, I certainly didn't feel that I belonged among them, or that I had earned this honor.

Mitt insisted, and the boys all backed him up. I began thinking about it, and while I wouldn't compare my battle with those of some of the other people who had been nominated, the chance to carry that torch really meant something to me. It would be my personal victory. I finally agreed, but only if Mitt joined me. I wanted it to be a family celebration.

Now all I had to do was run it. At the time Mitt nominated me, I really couldn't run. But I started to train for it. It was only about a fifth of a mile; I knew I could do it. I immediately put on my tennis shoes, got a water bottle, got on the treadmill, and ran for . . . one minute. That was it, one minute. That definitely wasn't going to work. The next day, I ran for two minutes, or as I liked to tell myself, twice as long as the day before. I was determined to do this. For weeks beforehand, I jogged and walked as much as I could, trying to increase my distance just a little every day. I had a path that I ran and walked and I would push myself to go a few steps farther every day. Once I had been able to run 5Ks without too much difficulty; now I was counting every single step. Believe me, I didn't hear the stirring theme from *Chariots of Fire* in my head as I ran, just my exhausted breath. But whatever it took, I pushed myself.

After I had been doing this every day for several weeks, my sister-in-law came out for a visit and we went hiking in the mountains. At one point I noticed she was breathing hard, almost panting, and I thought, *Wow, I'm the one with MS and I'm doing better than she is.*

Of course, I wasn't carrying anything in my hand. And there was no one on the sidelines watching me.

My run was to take place on the sixty-fifth and last day of the torch relay. By the time it reached Salt Lake, the torch had become a symbol of American resilience after the attacks of 9/11. Heroes had carried it through Ground Zero in New York, past the Pentagon in Virginia, and by the field outside of Shanksville, Pennsylvania. Along every mile of the route, people had stood on the sides, often waving American flags, while the runners in their own way paid tribute before handing the torch to the next bearer.

By the time the flame got to me, it had traveled by cars, planes, ships, trains, dog sleds, skis, snowmobiles, ice skates, and even sleighs. Americans had cheered, saluted, and often cried. All Americans then were sharing the enormous pain caused by the 9/11 attacks, and the relay played a small role in the healing process. We would actually help bring the torch into Salt Lake City. I was thrilled to be able to do that. Mitt and I had moved to Utah so he could try to untangle the Olympics and I could try to recover from my disease. During the three years we were in Salt Lake City, the residents had given us so much that I really was thrilled to be carrying the torch into the city.

The first thought that came into my mind when I was handed the Olympic torch on a residential street in East Salt Lake City was probably the same thought as the almost twelve thousand people who had carried it before me: *Don't drop it!*

I grasped it tightly in my right hand, held it up triumphantly, and began jogging. I was so psyched up for that moment that I took right off—leaving Mitt, Josh, and his wife, Jen, standing there dumfounded. Where did that energy come from? I was running almost completely on adrenaline. Josh quickly caught up with me. "Mom?" he yelled.

"I can do it!" I yelled right back at him, "I can do it!" That stretch seemed like the longest distance I had ever run, and also the shortest. My little run took forever and seemed to last a second. As I ran, I saw all my friends from Margo's barn cheering me on. Her children were holding a sign, "We Love You, Ann!" It was a glorious moment, and I was deeply touched.

I wasn't as invincible as I had hoped to be, though. Toward the end, I started getting tired. That torch was getting mighty heavy. Mitt reached over and helped me hold it up, and that's the way we finished our portion of the run together. It was so appropriate.

There was one more piece of Olympic business to be done. While rodeo had been an official event in the 1988 Calgary Winter Olympics, to honor the great American West the three-day America versus Canada Olympic Command Performance Rodeo was being held as part of Salt Lake's Olympic celebration, but not part of the Games. Margo, Jan, and I had been invited to demonstrate some dressage techniques during a pause in competition. For this event, I was riding a relatively new horse, named Baron. Baron had taken the place of Buddy. Buddy had helped me get through the basics of dressage; that was his skill level. But as I progressed beyond that, I needed a new teacher, and that was Baron.

I sometimes called Baron "Professor," because of the way he patiently took me to the next level. Had he been human, he would have worn horn-rimmed glasses, a tweed jacket, and a bow tie. Buddy had been my training wheels. Baron was a full-fledged two-wheeler.

As Margo, Jan, and I huddled beneath the bleachers, listening to the crowd roaring and waiting to go on, it did occur to me how wonderful and unpredictable life can be. Only a few years earlier I had been in the midst of a deep depression, wishing I would be struck by a disease that would kill me quickly rather than slowly losing control of my body. I had been grasping for any hope. Now here I was crammed uncomfortably into a small area with two friends and two nervous horses waiting to perform basic dressage in front of a large and loud crowd.

I wasn't cured—I knew there was not yet a cure for MS—but I was well along the road to recovery, and knew that my disease was manageable. I had learned so much, and I was so incredibly grateful.

"That's ten minutes," the rodeo director warned us. "Got it?" It seemed clear from his tone of voice that he resented our intruding on his rodeo. I suspected he had been told that "Mitt Romney's wife" was going to ride an exhibition during a break in competition and resented having to accommodate me. He was pulling rank a little, reminding us that we had ten minutes and only ten minutes to perform.

"Got it. Thanks!" I yelled back.

This exhibition was far from a normal dressage competition. Normally the arena is quiet, to allow the horse and rider to communicate without distraction. Any loud noise or unexpected movement can shatter the concentration, so much so that the normal dressage audience doesn't respond until the horse has left the arena. Rodeos are entirely different. It's cowboy time, and everyone is cheering loudly for their roper or rider. The exhibition center was packed with Americans and Canadians rooting for their home team. Jan was very concerned about our horses; they'd been transported from the barn to the arena on a freezing cold and very dark February night, after getting caught in a traffic jam of countless cars. Four helicopters had been hovering above the van, only adding to the confusion. At the arena the horses were led into a strange environment and exposed to sudden and great bursts of noise.

While Jan was confident he could handle his own horse, I knew he was concerned about me. Horses are big and very strong animals, and if my horse bolted, I could really be hurt. I'd been fine rehearsing in the tranquility of Margo's barn, but this was a raucous situation.

When the rodeo manager told us we were on, Jan looked at me and asked, "You ready for this, yah?"

"I'll be fine," I said. But Baron was restless, moving nervously. I was sure he'd settle down when I got on him, but it was that "getting on" that presented the problem. It took three people to hold him still enough for me to mount. That had never been necessary before. I patted him on the neck and said a few words, hoping my familiar voice would calm him.

With a last glance at Jan, Margo and I rode into the arena. Unlike the cowboys in competition, we were dressed in the formal regalia of dressage, from white breeches to white gloves, including the traditional long black Shadbelly riding coat. Fortunately, Mitt was going to provide the explanation for our exhibition—and after what Mitt had done to turn the Olympics into a rousing success, he was considered a hero. So when he spoke, people paid full attention.

"What you're seeing Ann do here is a piaffe," he explained, "which is simply a calm, elevated trot in place." Had I not been quite so nervous I would have enjoyed his commentary. It wasn't very long ago that Mitt wouldn't have known the difference between a piaffe and a pianissimo. But when he accepted the fact that riding had become my passion, he started joining me at Margo's barn on occasion. While I was training, he'd be helping out in the barn, washing down horses, driving horse trailers, even mucking the stalls. Mitt may have thought he knew what he was getting into when we made the decision to leave Boston to come to Salt Lake, but he couldn't possibly have anticipated what he was stepping into, literally, as he mucked Margo's stalls!

My part in the exhibition ended without incident. Nobody in that audience recognized the little mistakes I made. And when I rode back beneath the bleachers and handed off the horse to Jan, who with Margo would demonstrate several of the most complex maneuvers, he looked at me with a smile on his face and paid me the greatest compliment I could have received: "Very good job."

Very good job. Those three words perfectly summed up the magical three years Mitt and I had spent in Salt Lake City.

Five

THERE WAS ONE OTHER ELEMENT that contributed greatly to my recovery. And I was reminded of it while riding Baron through a very early morning mist. In dressage, the rider communicates his or her commands by applying subtle pressure with the inside leg and the outside rein. In a true partnership between horse and rider, the horse will respond to those commands, completely trusting the rider.

That morning, a mountain wind was blowing the mist, creating a very spooky atmosphere. Baron was clearly uncomfortable. He was slightly disoriented. Baron was a wonderful horse, but on occasion a switch flipped and he became difficult to control. This was one of those times. He was being very impulsive, paying little attention to my commands. He was concerned about his safety, he wanted to bolt. This was a large, powerful animal, so I was wary and careful—and very frustrated. I was sitting tall and I could see everything that was going on around us for quite a distance. I could see all the dangers that might lie in our path. I thought, *Oh Baron, if you could only see the bigger picture you would be quiet and listen to the outside rein. Then everything would be fine.*

Then I had this sudden realization: Oh my gosh, this must be how God looks down on us. He does see the bigger picture. He knows what's right for us. We just need to be quiet and listen to His outside rein.

Of course I knew it was a parable, but it was cool. Jesus taught the shepherds with their sheep and lambs, and I was being taught through my horse how important it is to listen and maintain my faith in God. How important it was to listen to the outside rein and be confident that He does see the bigger picture.

There was a time during this period when I almost forgot that.

Faith is such an interesting concept, and it may have very different but equally important meanings to different people. There have been people who have suggested that there was a greater reason I was diagnosed with MS, and that it put me on a long trail that has had many positive ramifications. I've never believed that. I think life is almost indiscriminate. I've never believed that there was a master plan. I don't think I was given this disease because I would do something good because of it. I think life hits us all, and then we have to make choices. And hopefully all of us will find a place where we can make a positive difference.

It took me a long time to understand that. My father's religion was the amazing uniformity of nature. He believed that there had to be some master engineer who fit all the pieces together, but then confidently left his invention to run on its own. Growing up, I needed more of an explanation than that. There was a part of me that believed there had to be more than that. I didn't know what it was, I didn't know where to find an answer, and I most certainly did not want to disappoint my father. But there was a void in me that needed to be filled.

To be honest, when Mitt and I were dating, religion was not the first thing on his mind. It probably wasn't second or third, either. While he answered my endless questions, he never tried, in any way, to convince me that his religion, the Mormon Church, was better than or different from any other religion.

While admittedly I was curious about it, I was sixteen years old, and in the spring and summer of 1965, I had many other interests. Within months of meeting Mitt, I was deeply in love with him. We'd go out at night and Mitt would always make sure to get me home at a reasonable hour. My parents liked him right away. And when I got home, I'd kiss my parents good night, shut my bedroom door, turn out the lights—and crawl out my first-floor window to meet Mitt, who was waiting around the block. We'd spend several more hours together and then I'd sneak back into my house. My parents never knew that part about Mitt.

At his senior prom, Mitt led me outside and asked me to marry him. We professed our eternal teenage love for each other, and I said yes, but we were young and knew that marriage was far off. As I've mentioned, it is a tradition in the Church of Jesus Christ of Latter Day Saints that young men and, more recently, women volunteer for a two-year mission to do good deeds and spread the faith. While expected, it is not mandatory. Yet Mitt and I agreed that if we were going to spend our lives together, it would be without any regrets over things we hadn't done. There would be no if-onlys in our life. Mitt went to France and, as it turned out, I went to church.

My father had great respect for Mitt's father, Michigan governor George Romney. So he allowed me to go to church with the Romneys. That was my introduction to organized religion.

The Mormon Church has a long and fascinating history, and many Americans know little about it except that at one point it recognized polygamy, or allowing a man to have several wives. Basically, Mormonism is a Christian faith that follows the teachings of Christ. Mormons believe that Jesus Christ is our savior and will redeem us from sin. Like every other religion, it has certain rules, known as the Words of Wisdom. Among them are restrictions on drinking alcohol, coffee, and tea; smoking; and engaging in premarital sex. At least part of the reason for this is to maintain a healthy body. But there also is the reality that making a commitment to follow certain tenets allows you to get so much more in return. Giving up something or following dietary codes is pretty much a part of every major religion, and as I found, Mormonism is no different. As in every other religion, members of the church follow the rules that best support their personal beliefs.

Mitt has always found the humor in this. At a formal

dinner one night while he was governor of Massachusetts, he looked around at the well-dressed people in attendance and admitted, "Usually when I get invited to gatherings like this one, it's just to be the designated driver."

Several years later, during the 2012 presidential campaign, he was asked how to prepare for a presidential debate. He considered the question, and then explained, "First, refrain from alcohol for sixty-five years before the debate."

I think what appealed to me most about the Mormon Church is the emphasis it places on the importance of family. Nothing is more important than the family unit. We believe that we are on earth to learn how to temper our passions and that our experiences, both good and bad, teach us those things that we need to learn, and that one day we will live again as a family unit, that families are eternal. This makes it easier to deal with hardships, because we believe they are only temporary and will ultimately prove to be positive.

I found a certain level of contentment within the Church that seemed to fit me well. I made a personal decision that I wanted to become part of this religion. I don't think my father liked it. He thought that organized religion was the cause of a lot of grief in the world. He wouldn't stop me from making my own decision, but he certainly wasn't supportive. The only thing he asked was that I not make any decision about religion until I was eighteen. With his permission, George Romney arranged for missionaries from the Church to come to our house and instruct me in the faith. Of course, what we didn't know was that my younger brother, Jim, would go into the living room before each meeting, hide under the couch, and listen silently. It turned out that he was as interested in finding his faith as I was.

Mitt didn't want me to convert because of him; he wanted to make sure I was doing it for myself. But in 1966, with Mitt away on his mission, I asked George Romney to baptize me. It is accurate to say that I became a Mormon, but on some level I was already a member of the faith. It just seemed to adhere so well to what I already believed deep inside. It actually was a pretty scary thing for me to do; it was so different from anything involving my high school friends, but I wasn't going to let anyone deter me. I had taken all the lessons, so I understood completely what I was embracing. I don't know how I knew this was the right path for me, but I knew it, and I had no doubts about it. My baptism took place in a church in Bloomfield Hills, and afterward I felt completely content, as if I had arrived at the place where I was supposed to be going.

While my father accepted my decision, he finally objected when my then-fourteen-year-old brother, Jim, said he also wanted to be baptized, and when, a surprise to all of us, my rebellious older brother, Rod, also independently took missionary lessons and was baptized while studying in England. My brother Jim joined the church as well, but not until he was eighteen. Many years later the biggest surprise was a phone call from my cancer-stricken mother. Since my father's death several months earlier, she had been struggling. Like Mitt and me, she and my father had spent most of their lives together, and his loss had devastated her. "You'd better sit down," she said. "I have two things to tell you. I'm dying, Ann. I can tell I don't have much time left." I didn't breathe. Those are the worst possible words a child can hear. Then she continued: "And I need to be baptized before I die."

I didn't know how to respond to that. Having just heard the most awful thing possible, it was difficult to find anything to say, but this wonderful feeling came over me. "That's wonderful," I finally managed to blurt out. And it was, it was.

Her words were stunning. My mother had always been a spiritual woman, but this—this could not possibly have been more unexpected, or appreciated.

I flew down to Florida the following weekend. My mother wanted to be baptized by my brother, Jim. There are few things more meaningful than watching a parent being baptized by her child. I watched as my mother grabbed on to the railing and stepped down into the warm water where Jim was waiting. Jim had the biggest smile on his face. She waded slowly into the water and reached out to him for support. He took her hand.

He said really loudly, maybe making sure that they could hear him in heaven, "Having been commissioned of Jesus Christ, I baptize you in the name of the Father, and of the Son, and of the Holy Ghost. Amen." Then he lowered her into the water, and we welcomed her into the faith.

My mother was so filled with joy. At one point she took hold of the bishop's hand and promised him, "I'm going to be the most active member of your congregation."

After the baptism, Jim and I remarked that we had felt our father's presence at the ceremony. Religion had always been such a sensitive issue in our home, and this seemed a resolution to that conflict.

A few days later, I went back to Boston. I was still at Logan Airport when my brother Rod called and told me to get back to Florida as quickly as possible. "She's barely hanging on," he said. I made it back in time to say good-bye. I remember how completely serene she looked, how angelic as she walked to eternity. Her decision to be baptized had brought us all a great feeling of acceptance and peace. We knew she was going to be in good hands, and that we would be reunited in heaven.

It really is amazing what a central role my faith has played in my life. Mitt was still on his mission in France when his father was deciding whether to run for the 1968 Republican presidential nomination. He took me with him on a campaign trip to Utah, the first political campaign trip of my life. Among our stops was the campus of Brigham Young University, a sprawling, beautiful setting in the Utah Valley, surrounded by snowcapped mountains. While many of my friends applied to the great Michigan universities, I had enrolled at B-Y-Woo, as students called it because so many of them married people they met there. I suppose one reason I picked it was that it made me feel closer to Mitt. But more than that, it was my introduction to the Mormon religion and culture. It took some getting used to; religion had been an interest of mine, I was very curious about it, but it had never been a core part of my life. My first Sunday at BYU, I was surprised to learn that just about all the students attended church every single Sunday, that those students built their lives around their religious values.

My brother Rod and me with our Welsh grandparents (Royal Oak, Michigan, 1950)

Rod and me with Mom and Dad (Royal Oak, Michigan)

Me at seven years old with my brothers Jim and Rod. Have you noticed I grew up with all boys and have all sons?

Rod, me, Jim, Mom, and Dad during my senior year of high school

High school BFFs, Sue Brethen
and Pam Hayes

Mom, Dad, and me with my college
buddies Cindy Davies and Jamie
Roehner (December 1967)

Me as a silly teenager

Ready for my junior prom, with Mitt

This came from Mitt, my missionary in France, reminding me that he still cared.

Another reminder from Mitt while on his mission in France

Mitt's senior prom. The night of his first proposal.

Our engagement photo (1969)

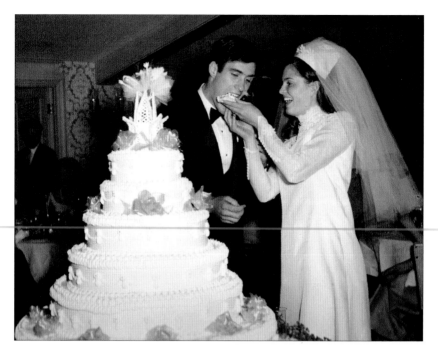

Always feeding my man. At our hometown wedding. (Bloomfield Hills, Michigan, March 21, 1969)

Throwing my bouquet at our hometown wedding

Our ceremony at the temple in Salt Lake City (March 22, 1969)

With our first son, Tagg (Provo, Utah, 1970)

Me with my youngest, Craig (1982)

At the beach with Tagg and Matt, our second son (Massachusetts, fall of 1972)

Mitt and I after apple picking with the boys in Massachusetts (c. 1985)

Perils of big brother babysitters. Craig covered in Fluff.

With my three youngest: Josh, Ben, and newborn Craig (1981)

I spent part of my second semester in France, studying the language in the village of Les Auberge, just outside Grenoble. That was the closest Mitt and I had been to each other in a year, but mission rules prohibited us from even seeing each other for a date or dinner. Apparently, the Church wanted young people on a mission to focus on their responsibilities, not their social life. It is intended to be a time for growth, when you experience new challenges.

One of those challenges was to our relationship. It's incredibly difficult for two young people to maintain a relationship when they don't see each other for two and a half years. After I returned to BYU, Mitt and I wrote regularly, but a letter a week is no substitute for togetherness. New experiences were filling my life, and the old ones, which included my years with Mitt, were being displaced. I had a difficult time even remembering what he looked like. This isn't unusual. High school romances rarely survive the separation of different colleges, much less different continents. I was completely honest with Mitt, telling him as gently as possible that I'd started dating other people, including the star of the basketball team. It wasn't quite a "Dear Mitt" letter, but it certainly wasn't a profession of my deep and eternal love, either.

We couldn't even fight about breaking up! Mitt wrote back a calm, understanding letter telling me that he loved me and hoped desperately that I would wait for him. Maybe some young women would have been angry at him for not being angry, but I wasn't. Mitt poured out his heart. I could feel his love in those pages. The maturity in his words reminded me that he was the most extraordinary young man

I'd ever known—even if he wasn't much of a basketball player. He had an unshakable core that allowed him to deal with the challenges of life. Maybe at that time I didn't quite understand where it came from. While I made him no promises, I knew I would wait for him.

When he returned home in December 1968, I met him at the airport with his family. I was afraid it would be like meeting a stranger, but instead the most wonderful thing happened. He walked through the gate, walked right past his parents, his sisters, his nieces and nephews, and embraced me. It was as though those two and a half years evaporated instantly. We were as close and as connected as the day he left. There were dozens of family members at the airport, but we had eyes only for each other. We climbed into the third-row seat of an Oldsmobile Vista Cruiser for the drive home. When the hour-long trip was over, we shocked everyone by informing them that we had waited long enough and we were getting married in three weeks. You can imagine how that went over. The next day, Mitt and I walked into my home to find both sets of parents, arms crossed, brows creased, and jaws set. I loved Mitt's dad forever for cracking a smile. He clearly was enjoying watching young love at work. We compromised and waited four months.

Our wedding was far more lavish than either of us wanted. It really was more for our parents than for us. Mitt and I just wanted to get married and get on with our lives. But that wasn't possible. George Romney was a very prominent man; he had been the popular governor of Michigan, a presidential candidate, and a Cabinet member, so our wedding became a large social event. But as I eventually learned, for my mother it had an even more special meaning. Several years later, we were in my kitchen when suddenly, for no apparent reason, she burst into tears. I couldn't imagine what had caused that—and then she explained: "I've never told you this, Ann," she said. "But when I got pregnant with you, your brother was only a few months old. I didn't know how I could handle it. Your dad and I decided we would have an abortion. We made arrangements to have it done abroad because it was illegal here. I had my tickets, my luggage was packed, and I was ready to go. But I got so sick that I couldn't go, and after that I knew I couldn't do it. And . . . and I can't believe what joy you've brought into our lives. When I think how close I came . . ."

I'm certain that this was on her mind as Mitt and I walked down the aisle on our wedding day.

Mitt and I were very happy to get away from all that attention on our honeymoon. I can remember wondering about our future. There were so many wonderful possibilities. Then Tagg came into our lives. Many people might not believe this, but Tagg was the first baby I ever held in my arms. I had grown up in the country, and there were no children around; my cousins were all my age, and I'd never even been a babysitter. So it was the most frightening thing to me when two weeks after we brought Tagg home, my mother decided to leave. "You can't leave me with this baby," I told her. "I don't know what to do with it."

She looked at Mitt and me and said, "Oh, you'll figure it out."

Mitt literally had to teach me how to change a diaper.

Growing up in a large Mormon community, he'd had a lot of experience with babies. I learned quickly, though. I had to, to survive. I remember so very vividly going for walks at night with our new baby. It was May. The lilacs were in full bloom and their fragrance just filled the air. The sky was filled with stars, and I was so happy I could have burst with joy. It was an idyllic time, and when I focus on it I can still smell those lilacs.

But life isn't always as simple as a peaceful walk on a beautiful May night. I've heard people use the expression "our faith was tested." That was never true of us. Instead, it was our faith that helped us get through several difficult times. For example, our then-ten-month-old son Ben's illness shook me and reminded me how vulnerable we all are. In an unbelievable tragedy, my aunt and uncle and their eight-year-old daughter were killed in a fire set by a deranged arsonist. And in 1992, when our youngest son, Craig, was ten years old and we were convinced we were done forever with diapers, I became pregnant again.

This was at the same time both my parents were suffering from what would be terminal cancers, and our son Tagg was planning his wedding. We were on an emotional roller coaster, never knowing whether the next phone call was going to be wonderful or sad news. When I began showing, we talked about the irony with our friends. "Being pregnant in your son's wedding is downright tacky," someone said. But before that could happen, I miscarried.

As we went through each of those experiences, and the many others of normal life, we relied on our faith. Throughout our marriage Mitt had remained very active in our church in Boston, for a long time spending as many as thirty hours weekly involved in church activities. In the Mormon religion we rely on lay clergy, people who volunteer their time to the church. Mitt served as a teacher, counselor, and leader; he chaperoned teen groups on trips; we sang together in the annual church musical and went caroling at Christmas; he worked with others on church business and finances. In 1982 he became a bishop of the church. Mitt's father had served as stake president, or leader of the Mormon Church, in Detroit; and in 1986 Mitt became president of what is known as the Boston Massachusetts Stake, serving in that role for eight years. So while Mitt and I did not try to make our religious beliefs an integral part of his political campaigns, our faith has always played a central role in our lives.

In some ways, Mitt's expression of belief actually is similar to my father's. As Mitt has said, he doesn't know when God intervenes in the affairs of humankind. He tends to believe that God lets us go about our life's work, and while He may weep when He sees people He loves suffering, He doesn't always step in and stop bad things from happening to good people. He doesn't always cure the sick or heal the afflicted. He doesn't get involved in business or financial affairs; He isn't going to get someone a promotion. Mitt says to pray as if it's up to God and act as if it's up to you.

To illustrate this, he often tells a story about one of the leaders of our Church, Brigham Young. It was Brigham Young who led the wagon train of Mormons into the West, finally reaching the Salt Lake. It was a tortuous and deadly journey. Once, as the wagons crossed the North Platte

River, one of them became caught in the current and was about to be swept away. It was carrying provisions for several families. The wagon driver dropped to his knees and began praying for God to save him and the wagon. Brigham Young rode his horse into the river, grabbed the man by the scuff of his neck, and pulled him up, telling him, "This is no time for prayer! Grab the reins!"

We had moved to Salt Lake City, the center of the Mormon Church, because Mitt was offered the Olympics job, but it also turned out to be essential to me. Although I had left a support group behind in Boston, I found a new and welcoming world in Utah. Boston is a wonderful city; we always will love it and be grateful for everything that happened there. We're Bostonians; we were educated there, we raised our family there, some of them still live there, many of our closest friendships were made there, and the world-renowned Boston hospitals that made all the difference in my life are there. But when we moved to Salt Lake City for the Olympics, it was as if we'd moved in with family.

For the first time, most of the people I was dealing with on a daily basis shared my religious beliefs, and this simply created a comfortable environment for me. Margo, for example, is Mormon. *That is unbelievable*, I thought. Back east, nobody I'd known professionally or worked with at any level had shared my faith before. But here everyone around me was Mormon: the police officers, the shop owners, the sanitation workers. I felt surrounded by a big family. While I know that Margo and I would have become close whether or not we shared a faith, that common bond certainly expedited the process. We would spend hours talking about the eternal perspectives. Although in a million years I never would have predicted it, moving to Salt Lake made being sick easier.

My faith proved essential after my diagnosis. I didn't look to it to explain why I had MS. When I wondered *Why me?* I never expected to hear an answer. I didn't believe that my getting MS was part of some master plan. It simply was part of my journey through life. But that faith sure came in handy in several different ways. Dr. Weiner is a strong believer in the powers of hope and optimism. He always tells other physicians to leave patients with hope, and my conviction that God loved me was that and more.

It is a teaching in our faith that if you become seriously ill, you may ask two or more priesthood holders to place their hands on your head and pronounce a blessing of healing. We believe that if it is God's will that you are healed, and if you have sufficient faith, you will in fact be healed. In some cases, this may happen in an immediate and miraculous way, as Christians of all faiths believe it did many times in the New Testament. My experience has been that healings from these priesthood blessings can also be less immediate, but just as miraculous.

Soon after arriving in Utah, I asked Mitt and Henry Eyring, one of his cousins and also a priesthood holder in our church, to give me a blessing of healing. In addition to their placing their hands on my head, Elder Eyring spoke words, much like a prayer. He said that my sickness would help me draw closer to Jesus Christ, to better understand His condescension to live among mankind, and to more fully appreciate His enormous sacrifice for us. He said that I would go through a healing process and that I would be guided to find people who would ease that path.

There is no question in my mind that Dr. Weiner and Fritz Blietschau were among the people that the blessing promised. I am also convinced that God has helped me recover much of my good health. I acknowledge the hand of God in every good thing in my life, while at the same time I know that in some cases He may not have actually pulled the strings that made those good things happen. One might argue that my improved health was the result only of Dr. Weiner's medical treatment, or only of Fritz's reflexology, or only of my genes, or only of my blessing by priesthood holders of my church. But I believe that all these things are connected, and I am thankful for each of them.

Some people reading this will understandably say that my improved health came about in part because of what I believed. I don't have a problem with that. In fact, that may be one way that God works to heal us. The brain is the greatest computer ever known; we still don't understand why things suddenly go wrong or, in many instances, what to do about it, but we also don't really understand the powers of the brain. We don't know what part hope and optimism play in the physiological as well as psychological treatment of a disease. I got my hope and my optimism from my faith. Beth Myers, our friend who served as Mitt's chief of staff while he was governor, has had to deal with her own challenging medical issues. We've talked about it, and as she reminded me, "You can't just rely on medicine, and you can't just sit in a ball—although certainly that's tempting. What you really need to do is make certain that your body, mind, and soul are all working together to reach the best possible outcome."

I was waging a full-scale battle against my disease. Dr. Weiner was taking good care of my body. My horseback riding and reflexology were taking care of my mind. When I was with Margo or Fritz, I would forget my illness and focus directly on the task at hand. But it was my faith that soothed my soul. It was my faith that allowed me to be at peace and to have confidence I would get better. While I was worried about the future, I was never angry and I never, ever gave up hope. I prayed. Mostly in my prayers I gave thanks for all the blessings I had been given and asked for the strength to deal with my challenges. Prayer has always been an important part of Mitt's and my life, a way of reminding us that we are united with a higher power. When we pray we don't generally ask for material things for ourselves, but in times of crisis we have asked for guidance and the wisdom to understand how to navigate troubled waters.

For me, prayer has always been a time for personal meditation, when I slow down everything going on around me to the point where I can simply listen. At that point, I can hear those things that don't have a voice or are normally drowned out by the clatter of life. Prayer gives me the time to be quiet and be completely present in the moment. It takes me to a place where everything around me dissolves: no worries, no cares, just in the moment.

In our Church, we believe that the Bible is scripture, the word of God. We also believe that God has inspired another book of scripture, the Book of Mormon, which gives an account of an ancient people who came to the

Americas from Jerusalem. And we believe that some of the writings of our Church's founder, Joseph Smith, were also inspired by God. Among these is one of Mitt and my favorite scriptures. Doctrine and Covenants, Section 90, verse 24, reads, "Search diligently, pray always and be believing, and all things shall work together for your good." That promise has always comforted and reassured me.

Less than two weeks after the Winter Olympics closing ceremonies, Salt Lake hosted the Winter Paralympics, in which eleven hundred handicapped athletes from thirty-six different countries competed in five winter sports. Coincidentally, the theme of the Paralympics was "Awaken the Mind, Free the Body, Inspire the Spirit." Mind, body, spirit. When Mitt welcomed the participants and spectators to "the friendliest place on the entire planet," he said they should feel at home in Salt Lake because "Here, the human spirit has dreamed and built, it has strived and achieved . . . You reawaken in us the spirit of this place. Welcome home."

Like most other people fighting a life-changing condition, my focus had been pretty narrow: me. But with my own disease in at least temporary remission, I began to look out at the world from a very different perspective. I had crossed a line and I would never again go back. I don't think I identified with the Paralympic athletes. I knew I didn't have either their handicaps or their skills, but I did understand their struggles. And I became their greatest cheerleader. We were out there every day to root for them. And while I believed that the old cliché "just by participating you win" was true, it was clear these athletes didn't think so. They were there to win, and they competed that way. It was impossible not to admire their determination.

The person I got to know best was sit-skier Chris Waddell, who would become the most decorated athlete in Paralympic history. We got to know each other making appearances to promote the games. Chris became the face of the Paralympics. He was the perfect choice: he was handsome, charming, outgoing, optimistic, and cheerful—and in 1998 he had been one of *People*'s 50 Most Beautiful People.

Chris had been paralyzed from the waist down in a skiing accident in 1988. He was a promising twenty-year-old ski racer when his ski popped off in the middle of a turn. In literally a split second, his life changed forever, but as he eventually came to believe, for the better. "If I hadn't had the accident, I never would have been the best at anything," he told a reporter. "That accident turned out to be the best thing that ever happened to me. I defined myself as a ski racer. That's what I was. But the accident forced me to look at myself differently."

The stories he told really affected me. He was an amazing athlete, and by the end of the decade he would climb Kilimanjaro's first 18,500 feet using a wheelchair that he operated himself, raising and lowering the wheels over rocks more than a foot tall. But only 840 feet from the top, he realized he couldn't make it. The terrain, the chair, the elements—it was all just too much. So he allowed members of his team to carry him to the top. It was an amazing feat, but for a time he felt like a total failure. Then he realized that accepting help is a defining aspect of living successfully in a society. "If I had done it alone," he told me, "it meant I wouldn't need anyone." That would have set him apart from others, which was precisely the thing he was determined that his wheelchair not be allowed to do. "I would be what I was trying to eliminate." One of the people on that climb said that Chris "made John Wayne look like a pansy."

Chris's lesson was reinforced a few days later, when the Czech team had some of its specially made skis and other equipment stolen. It was an unusually cruel thing to do. Those athletes couldn't afford to replace their equipment, and it looked as if they were going to have to go home without competing. But the word got out in Salt Lake, and suddenly people began contributing. They replaced the team's equipment, bought them new uniforms, put them up in their homes, and came out to the mountain to cheer for them. Spending time with Chris, with all the athletes, reminded me once again of that bag of rocks we all carry, although few of us actually carry it to the top of a mountain.

Another American athlete, Paralympic cross-country skier Mike Crenshaw, probably said it better than I can before the Games began, "As you go along, you realize that everyone's messed up somehow. Physically. Emotionally. Mentally. We've all got problems. It's a matter of what you do with them."

One of the recurring themes I heard from several athletes was the fact that they had found a way to take that bag of rocks and build something wonderful out of it. That doesn't mean they overlooked their situation. One of the Paralympic athletes told me that he hated the fact that he didn't have legs, but because he didn't he was experiencing things he could never have imagined. What Chris meant, what I learned, is that none of us had a choice in this. What happened to me happened, but eventually it brought me, all of us, to places I would never have found or gone without it.

What we all learned is how to build on our new foundation.

Having MS made me part of a large community of people who have crossed a line. For some people, like me, it was a slow journey—with aches and pains, numbness and balance issues, eventually leading to a diagnosis. For others, like Chris, it happened instantly—a bad turn, a distraction, being in the wrong place, an accident. But the end result is the same: life is changed forever.

As a member of this new club, I began to meet so many people who were able to teach me lessons about the human spirit. One of them was a woman I eventually got to know in Utah named Stephanie Nielson. As Stephanie explains, "There is a camaraderie of people [*sic*] who have been through very traumatic experiences. It doesn't matter what it is, we sort of cling to each other because we know what it feels like. We survived, and our stories connect us because of how we overcame things."

In reality, few people have overcome more than Stephanie. The way she went about doing it is similar to my own experience and, as I've learned, that of so many other people as they learned to deal with the weight they were carrying. Stephanie had already built up a considerable readership for her blog, *NieNie Dialogues*, her way of sharing her joy in being the mother of four small children and a member of the Mormon faith, when she and her husband,

Christian, and his flight instructor took off one afternoon in a small red-and-white Cessna from an airfield
in St. John's, Arizona. They were heading home to Mesa,
where she had left pizza dough on the counter that she
intended to bake for dinner. "We took off," she remembers,
"and we just weren't gaining altitude. Our landing gear
caught in power lines and got ripped off and we nosedived
into the ground. I can remember seeing my feet dangling
out of the airplane. It felt like the Flintstones. When my
plane was actually crashing down from the sky, I covered
my face and saw my children and I said a prayer, Oh God,
please don't take me right now. I don't want my children to
know that my last moments on earth were of fear."

The plane exploded in flames. The flight instructor, Doug
Kinneard, would pass away from his injuries. Christian
managed to get out of the burning plane and ran around
the other side to try to open the door. Stephanie woke up
and looked around:

*And I thought everyone left me. I was really frightened. I
could smell myself burning. I couldn't get my seatbelt off
because it was too hot. I started thinking about my kids; and
I thought, please let this happen to me fast. I know it's going
to hurt really bad for the next few minutes, then it will take
me and I'm ready for that. But then a miracle happened.*

*I sensed my grandmother, who had passed on several
years before, was there with me. "Calm down, Stephanie,"
she said. "Just lift that seatbelt off, push open the door." I
ran into a field and remembered that my third-grade
teacher had taught us to drop and roll. I did that. We had*

crashed into the yard of the bishop of the Mormon congre-
gation in that area, into a woodpile that burst into flames.
He came to help and I told him, "Can you please help me
get up. I have to get home. I have pizza dough waiting
on the counter and we're making pizza tonight."

There was little he could do to help; Stephanie had suffered burns over more than 80 percent of her body, including her face. Christian had burns over about 35 percent of
his body. Stephanie's heart stopped twice in the rescue helicopter racing her to a hospital. At best, pessimistic doctors
gave her a fifty-fifty chance of surviving. She was in a coma
for ten weeks, fighting infections, shock, twelve operations,
and unimaginable pain.

She woke up to her new life. The fire had disfigured her
face so badly that her children didn't recognize her.

I was so depressed I couldn't look in a mirror, but I could
see from the way other people were looking at me that
something was terribly, terribly wrong. My five-year-old
daughter was the first of my children to see me. She looked
at me and went as white as a ghost. She wouldn't look at
me again for five months. When she left my hospital room
I heard her tell the other kids, "Don't go in there, you don't
want to see Mom." My heart broke in half. I remember
thinking, just tell the kids that I died and send me to a
hospital far away. I went into a deeper depression.

There were times, she admits, that the depression and
pain were so unbearable that she prayed that she would die.

Stephanie's depression lasted more than six months. Then she experienced the first moment of joy. She was at home, lying on a couch. It was a magnificent fall day, and she looked outside and watched as a breeze simply blew the leaves. As those leaves fluttered, she realized she was alive; she had survived. And in her mind, she remembers:

I could see all of the other burn survivors I had known in the hospital. Most of them were not as badly burned as I was, but their injuries were worse. They didn't have fingers, or a nose. I had all my fingers, all my toes, all my limbs; I had a nose, I had a mouth and I could talk, my hair was growing, I had my children and our relationship was growing back, I have my husband who loves me and stuck by me, I have a huge group of people who pray for me and offer encouragement and I have a Father in Heaven who loves me. I get to be at my little girls' weddings. I realized, I have everything. I won't let this accident define me. And at that moment I decided, that's it. I'm not going to spend any more of my life sitting here feeling sorry for myself.

Her depression didn't just disappear. But the moments when she just forgot all about it continued to expand. Finally she began to set limits: "I told myself, okay Stephanie, you can have five minutes of just feeling sorry for yourself and crying and screaming. I was so mad at the situation. Well, at first it was twenty minutes, but over time I would make it less and less."

As with so many of us who have dealt with challenges,

there was the medicine that made her feel better, but prevented her from really feeling anything. The medicine numbed her senses. "It took away my depression, but it didn't help me feel." Weaning herself off those pain-killing medications was difficult. To accomplish that, Stephanie set out to regain her passions. With her hands still encased in gloves to keep scars from rising, she made a list of all the things that she had done before the accident that gave her pleasure. The list of things she loved to do included driving a car, making dinner, hiking up a mountain, tying her shoes, riding a bike, changing a diaper, riding a horse, and perhaps most difficult of all, having another child. Her goal became accomplishing everything on that list. Through the years she crossed them all off. It was a long series of small victories. Big and small, each had great meaning. "To cross off 'change a diaper' was such a great day for me," she writes. "Just being able to do the things that I had done before was so empowering to me."

Among the first things on her list was closing a Ziploc bag, and among the last was riding a horse. Stephanie, like me, had grown up riding. "I rode all the time when I was younger, but when we all got older my dad sold our horses. I hadn't been on a horse for years until my husband decided to give me riding lessons for my birthday. It was very hard, I had to adapt to everything. But more than anything, sitting on a horse as I had done when I was a little girl just made me feel normal. Everybody's normal is different; for me it is being Mom, a wife and a mother, and riding a horse."

It took her several years to regain control of her body.

For some time after the accident she was scared even to walk up a flight of stairs, frightened that she would fall and be unable to protect herself. But eventually her fears became too limiting; they were preventing her from living, so she forced herself to climb the stairs and took small steps forward. She would stretch her new skin by practicing yoga. There was a secluded path behind her house, and she would walk and jog there, going a little bit farther each day, until finally it came time to hike up the mountain. Her plan was to make the climb on the first anniversary of the plane accident, as a way to celebrate her recovery.

This particular mountain is known as Y Mountain. It is called that because about halfway up, a large white concrete Y serves as a reminder that the mountain overlooks Brigham Young University. Stephanie had climbed it many times, even running to the Y when she was pregnant. She had taken her children up there. But this would be the first climb of her new life. She climbed the 5,808-foot trail in forty painful minutes. It was, as she described it, "a beginning and an end."

Physically she continued to make slow progress; psychological progress was equally difficult. The memories were awful; sometimes she had to push them away. "There were nights when I couldn't sleep very well," she said. "I would lie there thinking how horrible this was and wonder why it happened to me. All I wanted to do was be a mom and raise my kids to be good citizens and this plane crash was just cramping all that. Then I began forcing myself to think about things that I was thankful for, and they totally outweighed the things I was going through. Pretty soon that list just grew and grew until instead of counting sheep I counted those things that brought me happiness."

In public, the accident was impossible to forget. At first she didn't want to leave the house. She would stay inside with the blinds closed. When she did go out, people would look at her reconstructed face strangely. She worried that as her children got older they would be embarrassed to be seen with her, that they would not want to bring their friends over. There wasn't much she could do about that, she knew.

There was still one more thing to accomplish on her list. She wanted to have another child. Eventually her doctors told her there was no physical reason why she shouldn't. She and Christian got pregnant. That in itself was a great victory. As the months passed, she embraced her new face, remembering that beauty starts inside. Once she felt that self-confidence, she stopped caring what other people thought of her. She says, "I would stand in front of the mirror and look at myself and think, you've been through something hard and you did it. And that's what's beautiful about me." Then one day, when she was about eight months pregnant, her son Oliver, who was in kindergarten, forgot his lunch. She knew she had to bring it to him. For most mothers, this is a simple errand; for Stephanie, it meant being seen by her son's classmates.

I got there during recess and they were all playing out-
side. I waved to him and he came running up to me and
three or four of his friends followed him. They kind of stood
back and were whispering to each other and I knew they

were wondering, what's wrong with Oliver's mom? I had heard those type of whispered remarks a lot. I handed Oliver his lunch and gave him a big hug and told him I'd see him at home. As I walked away one of Oliver's friends asked him, "What's wrong with your mom?"

Oliver got kind of a weird look on his face; he looked at me then looked at his friend and asked him, "Haven't you ever seen a pregnant mommy before?"

Working simultaneously on her body, mind, and spirit enables Stephanie to continue to deal with her challenges. Just as I had done, Stephanie also relied on her faith. When asked how she managed to get through it, she always begins by crediting God, but also always adds, "If you don't believe, the important thing is to find something bigger than you, bigger and brighter than you are. Surviving is so much easier when there is something you are reaching for."

NieNie Dialogues is now one of the most popular blogs online, with more than three million readers. Through her blog, Stephanie conveys the message she learned, the message that all of us, the Paralympic athletes and everyone who has been through a life-altering experience, have learned: You can get better. And what's really important is to look outward, not inward, and become a source of strength for others, helping them work through what you've already experienced. I get calls all the time from people who have been diagnosed with MS and other disease and give them much of the same advice I got.

Mitt and I frequently meet people who have been

through daunting challenges. We are continually inspired as we learn how they overcame those challenges to lead as full and as productive lives as possible. During Mitt's 2012 campaign for president, he met Sam Schmidt in Las Vegas. In January 2000, Sam's Indianapolis racing car hit the wall. This father of two young children spent five months on a respirator and was rendered quadriplegic; he can move nothing below his neck. He and Mitt spoke about his life since then: his morning begins with a two- to three-hour routine for bowel, bladder, teeth, shower, and dressing. That would be enough to make a lot of people give up. Instead, Sam owns and manages an Indy car racing team, which regularly dominates the Firestone Indy Lights, having won sixty races. And he himself has actually begun to drive again. He has a Corvette that has been outfitted with special controls. To accelerate, he blows in an air tube. To brake, he sucks the air out of it. To turn left or right, he looks carefully left or right, respectively. Accordingly, he warned his racing buddies, "You gotta keep the bikinis out of the grandstands, because you don't want any sudden movements."

Sam's disability is still there. He endures it every day, every hour. But that has not kept him from fully engaging in life.

Through the campaigns, through our work with different organizations, Mitt and I have met so many people who have carried their bag of rocks up a hill or into the winner's circle. While their challenges have included almost everything imaginable, there are similarities in the way people have dealt with them. Inevitably, it comes down to body, mind, and spirit.

By the conclusion of the Olympics and Paralympics, my disease was in remission—not cured, but in remission, which is a medical term for managed. It means it is under control, for now. Mitt and I had become accustomed to living with it, and making the necessary concessions, but we continued preparing for the possible. We knew it wasn't gone, it wasn't defeated, and that on occasion it would rise up and remind us, but we weren't going to allow it to dictate our choices in life. Mitt referred to our being irrationally hopeful.

He used to talk about his mother: "Every year she would gather us around her and tell us, 'I love you all very much, but this could be my last Christmas. I'm not well; this could be my last. Your father's so healthy and strong, but I have all these conditions.' That was her annual Christmas message. And the first few times we heard it we really worried about her. Of course, my mother lived to be eighty-nine, outliving my father by two years."

As we prepared to leave Salt Lake City, I remained irrationally hopeful.

Six

SEVERAL TIMES in the months leading up to the Opening Ceremonies, Mitt and I had paused to take a deep breath, look at each other and wonder, *what are we going to do next?* For the first time in our life we had no plans. After the Olympics ended, we could go anywhere and do anything we might choose. We didn't have to be anywhere, we didn't have to worry about getting the kids to school, and we didn't have to go to meetings or fulfill responsibilities. We were people who had spent our entire lives following schedules, racing to fulfill endless obligations, and suddenly we were going to have a life with absolutely nothing planned.

We were financially secure; with the exception of Craig, all our boys were on their own; and Mitt didn't have a business to run.

Neither of us was very good at doing nothing. We're the

kind of people who are happiest when we have to complain about being too busy. After spending years worrying if I even had a future, and then being given at least the possibility of a productive one, I certainly didn't intend to waste it. I needed to be involved in life. And Mitt could never be content watching life pass by. He's a problem solver, that's what he does, and I knew he would be lost if there were no problems to be solved. For some people, that type of life might sound ideal, but it didn't fit us.

Mitt's success in turning around the Olympics had attracted the attention of political professionals. Some people in Utah had asked him to consider running for governor of that state, but Utah wasn't our home, and it already had plenty of conservative talent. Kerry Healey, the chairperson of the Massachusetts Republican Party, quietly flew to Salt Lake to ask him to consider a run for governor. The then-governor of Massachusetts faced dim prospects for reelection.

There is a saying among people who have spent time in politics: if you have politics in your blood, get a vaccination! Mitt had politics in his blood. Many people remember that his father, George Romney, had been a very popular three-term governor of Michigan and a leading candidate for the presidency. It wasn't so much that he enjoyed politics, but he believed that being an elected official was a very good way of helping people. Fewer people remember that Mitt's mother also ran for political office. Lenore Romney was certainly a memorable woman. During George's presidential campaign, a reporter asked her to comment on the old saying "Behind every great man there is a great woman."

She didn't hesitate, replying, "I think that behind every great man there is a very surprised mother-in-law!" Lenore Romney won Michigan's Republican Senate primary in 1970 for the right to run against the popular incumbent, Philip Hart. Hart was so popular, in fact, that the Senate named its third office building in his honor. There was little chance she would beat him; in fact, years later Mitt would compare his own 1994 Senate campaign against the popular Ted Kennedy to his mother's unsuccessful effort. So while Mitt sat at the table with his father, he also learned politics from his mother, serving as her driver and advance man. Politics was in his blood on both sides.

I come from a political family too. My father was the first person in our family to win an election, when he became mayor of my hometown. In early 1977, I ran for a seat representing our precinct in the Belmont, Massachusetts, town meeting. The big issue was whether to move the fire station. I had placards printed with my picture and platform, walked around the neighborhood, and rang every doorbell. I won my election. Campaigning was hard for me: I was shy, but I found that when I really believed in something, I could overcome my hesitancy. As long as I was speaking from my heart, and I wasn't just saying things because I wanted to win, I didn't have any trouble expressing myself. That was to prove true years later, when I stood in front of thousands of people explaining why they should vote for my husband.

Both Mitt and his mother were realists, they knew how difficult it would be to win their campaigns, but both of them believed it was important to try to offer their messages. Mitt once compared running against Ted Kennedy in Massachusetts to being in a ski race against Jean-Claude Killy. Though, the only thing the two had in common is that they both went downhill fast. Mitt's 1994 race was a difficult campaign, and I received some criticism for being a little uncomfortable and out of touch. It was hard for me, and learning how to accept criticism was even more difficult. In fact, after we had lost the election, I told Mitt that this was the last time I was ever going to go through something like that. To paraphrase Mark Twain, I meant it so strongly that I've told him the same thing after every election.

After what we experienced during that 1994 Senate campaign, Mitt was reluctant to start another one in 2002. We would lose our private life, and everything we did or said would show up in the headlines. Years later, Mitt remembered having a dream in which he was trying to get out of a parking garage and the person in front of him seemed to take forever to pay. In this dream, Mitt got irritated and honked his horn, and the guy turned around to yell at him. Mitt got out of his car, and the two of them argued and then got back in their cars. It was the kind of thing that might actually happen—except, in the dream, the next day the entire encounter showed up on YouTube.

Politics is like a cage fight—only bloodier. The opposition tries to create the worst possible image of you. Once, for example, while Mitt was governor, we were on our annual family vacation at our summer home on Lake Winnipesaukee in New Hampshire. At about eight thirty in the evening, while Mitt, Josh, and Craig were putting everything away, they heard screams for help coming from somewhere offshore. They got on jet skis and raced out into the dusk. A family of six adults and a dog had been tossed into the water about three hundred yards from shore when their nineteen-foot wooden boat suddenly began taking on water. It sank in just minutes, and they'd been in the water for quite some time. They were wearing life jackets, so they weren't in danger of drowning, but because it was getting dark, they easily could have been hit by a passing speedboat. Mitt pulled two of them and the dog onto his jet ski and brought them back to shore, while Josh and Craig stayed on the scene. Two more trips brought the rest of the family to safety. Eventually we took them to their home across the lake.

Newspapers reported the story of the governor helping rescue a family in New Hampshire; and when he walked into his office a few days later, he found his staff had put a stuffed Scottie dressed in a bathing suit and a life preserver in his chair.

Mitt, Josh, and Craig hadn't gone into a burning building, but they had provided help in a potentially dangerous situation. But rather than acknowledging a good deed, the opposition party attacked: one state representative told the *Boston Herald*, "There are lots of people drowning in the Commonwealth right now who would certainly welcome a rescue." Another representative criticized us for vacationing in New Hampshire. "Other governors would have been condemned for leaving the state, but Romney seems to have privileges other governors haven't." And a party spokesperson added that Mitt, who had lived in Massachusetts for thirty years, "only chooses to run for office in Massa-chusetts. He doesn't vacation here." That was the criticism he received for rescuing people! If you've got thin skin, politics is not for you.

Also looming over our decision was the reality of my health. While my MS was in remission, we didn't know for certain the triggers that might lead to another attack. Nor did we know what the extent or severity of such an attack would be. That was an unknown we had gotten used to liv-ing with. But stress certainly might be a trigger, and as we had learned, there are few things more stressful, win or lose, than a political campaign. Running for political office, even on the state level, requires a total commitment of time and energy. It's more than a full-time job. There is no allowance for headaches or illness, no time to deal with personal or family issues. It's up early in the morning, put on a smile, and deal with whatever happens.

I had been speaking regularly with Dr. Weiner, so I called to ask him how a political campaign might affect me. Dr. Weiner has always been a voice of encouragement. He urges his patients to keep moving forward. He wants them to do as much as they can safely do. But there are some cir-cumstances where a line has to be drawn: he had a patient who was a Navy pilot, and after an MS attack the Navy wouldn't put him back in a cockpit. Still, the one trap Dr. Weiner urged his patients not to fall into was unneces-sarily limiting their lives. He did not want his patients to be afraid of living a full life. "Look, Ann," he told me. "I don't think this is going to cause a relapse. You can handle it. The one thing you have to be aware of is hitting the wall.

If you get tired you have to stop. Just tell whoever you have to tell that your batteries need to be recharged. But other than that, go for it."

We had a family meeting to make the final decision. Mitt believed there were things he could do as governor that would be important for the people of Massachusetts. The boys and their wives sat with Mitt and me, and we talked it out. I was ambivalent; while I believed Mitt would be an excellent governor, I didn't want to leave the life I had built in Utah so soon. I had recovered my health there; I loved riding, I loved being outdoors, I loved being with Margo and the girls in the barn. As much as I considered Boston home, I wasn't quite ready to go back. I was healthy in Utah, and Boston was where I had been sick.

While each member of the family has a vote, in reality some votes are more equal than others. My vote was the one that counted most. Mitt was clear: he would not go forward with a campaign if I thought it was going to be too much for me, or if it would have a negative effect on my health. It turned out there was unanimous agreement within the family: basically it was up to me. If my health permitted it, they were in favor of Mitt going after the nomination. Then they all looked to me. In so many different ways, Mitt and our boys each asked me if I really believed I was up to the stress of a political campaign.

In my heart I was probably the least inclined of everyone in the family to want to do it. I was in a happy place, and I knew that politics at times could get very ugly. I didn't want to go into a dark, scary place. My hesitation had nothing to do with winning—I could deal with a win or a loss.

I was much more concerned about uprooting myself from a supportive environment. But I knew it was something Mitt wanted to do, and something he could do very well. He could make a real difference in people's lives. My instincts told me this was the right thing to do.

Let's do it, I said—or something like that which conveyed a lot more confidence than I felt.

Massachusetts is a difficult state for a Republican running for political office. Democrats outnumber Republicans three to one. Mitt once joked, "Being a Conservative Republican in Massachusetts is a bit like being a cattle rancher at a vegetarian convention." But he had gained a tremendous amount of respect because of the job he'd done at the Olympics.

For Mitt, it was like jumping from one frying pan into another. He didn't take time to decompress; he just went into a different mode. Fortunately, there was no party primary, so it was a relatively brief campaign, and beyond some newspaper interviews there wasn't much for me to do. When Mitt moved back to Boston, I remained in Utah for several weeks. I just wasn't ready. Mentally, emotionally, and physically I just couldn't bear to leave my horses. I couldn't leave the mountains; I couldn't leave all the things that had kept me healthy and strong and go back to the place where I had gotten sick. So I didn't jump back into a campaign arena. I flew back to see Mitt on weekends, and then for a month, and then I screwed up my courage and decided it was time to go home for good.

But I needed to take my equine therapy with me. I shipped my horse back to Boston, and Margo and Jan both helped me find the right barn for him. In fact, Margo came back to Boston with me. I remember watching as she put my saddle in place in the new barn and realizing that the amazing experience I'd had in Salt Lake was really over. *Oh no, Margo,* I thought. *I can't do this without you, not without you being part of my life here.* I knew how incredibly hard it was going to be to adjust again. While everything about Boston was familiar to me—I knew every street and building—I was seeing it through my new eyes for the first time.

I was fortunate to be able to keep a reasonably low profile throughout the campaign. The reporters knew about my disease but didn't quite know how to handle it. It actually was a tricky issue; if the campaign brought it up, some people might believe we were looking for sympathy votes, but we couldn't pretend it didn't exist, either. Mitt's staff never developed a strategy for me. They didn't have to. I had learned my lessons in the Senate campaign. During that campaign I had been open and honest, and perhaps a little naïve. I certainly had a lot to learn about politics. I admitted that Mitt and I didn't fight with each other, I talked about having to lose weight, and I reminisced about our student days. I was turned into a cliché as journalists inaccurately equated my being a stay-at-home mother who'd raised five kids while loving her husband with being a so-called Stepford Wife, a robotic woman who existed only to serve her husband's needs. Those journalists should have spent one day with me when we had five boys in the house.

Throughout the campaign, I was very cautious. I took small steps, waiting to see how my body responded. And when I was comfortable, I took slightly bigger steps. I was gradually regaining my confidence. I attended some events with Mitt and made other low-key appearances by myself, but I was never heavily involved.

The biggest issue in the campaign was how to solve Massachusetts's fiscal problem. The state needed to raise several billion dollars to balance the budget. Mitt was a successful businessman, but he was running against a liberal Irish-Catholic woman in a liberal, Irish-Catholic state. The polls bounced around more than I had when I'd started riding again. In late September, after the Democratic nominating convention, Mitt was trailing by six points, but by Election Day, the race was too close to call. At that point there was nothing much more we could do. We went to bed the night before not knowing what to expect. Slightly over two million votes were cast, and Mitt won by more than a hundred thousand votes. Standing on the stage that night was one of the most memorable experiences of my life. We had come a long way. Only a few years earlier I'd thought there was nothing left for me, but since then, I'd carried the Olympic torch, and now I was standing with my husband to celebrate an important political victory. I was immensely grateful.

Mitt had won the election. Now all he had to do was get Massachusetts back on track. He had proven himself to be a great manager, but in running the state, he turned to what he had learned from his father: "I saw how he solicited advice from other people, how he built a team, how he made decisions based on data and analysis and solid thinking, not just gut feeling or opinion," Mitt says.

Following that example, the first thing Mitt did was to

put together a strong organization. Several people joined his administration who eventually would play an important part in our lives, among them Natalie Waczko and Beth Myers. Natalie was living in Toronto and working as a policy adviser for the Canadian government's Ministry of Tourism, Culture, and Sport when a friend of hers who was working on Mitt's 2002 campaign suggested she come to Boston. She'd visited Boston as a member of the Havergal College prep school rowing team to compete in the Head of the Charles Regatta and had liked it so much she wanted to find a way to come back. She joined the campaign. If you met Natalie, you loved Natalie, period. She had a wonderful, infectious laugh. Just describing her makes me smile: She was spontaneous, joyful, silly at times, and fun to be with. She seemed to get a kick out of life.

On the job, she was the exact opposite: She was a no-nonsense, get-the-job-done, no-foolishness kind of person who was able to get the things done that needed to be done and do so without making anybody angry or upset. While she was working on the campaign, she met Bradley Crate, and they fell in love. They tried to hide it, but they fooled exactly nobody, and we all were thrilled for them. Eventually they got married and had a little girl, Helena.

When Mitt took a look at his new office, he realized it was in pretty bad shape. Dark drapes were torn, and blinds were broken. Curtain rods were missing or bent. Paint was peeling from the walls. The furnishings were spartan: sufficient but quite a bit less than might be expected for a state's chief executive. A lot of repair work was needed, but there was no money to do it. Because Massachusetts was in financial difficulty, there weren't funds to pay for necessities, much less to make office repairs or improvements. There certainly was no money in the budget for the First Lady's office! In fact, I didn't have an office, and I didn't have a single staff person. Natalie ended up wearing two hats, one as Mitt's assistant and gatekeeper. If you wanted to see him, you had to go through her, and he trusted her judgment to decide whom was important for him to see and whom she should steer him away from. The second hat she wore was as my assistant. Together, we spruced up Mitt's office.

Natalie was in charge of scheduling for both Mitt and me. She scheduled events I needed to attend and often went with me to them; she became invaluable to both of us. In due course, we became good friends. I grew to love her like a daughter.

One of the causes we worked together on was raising funds for horse therapy; we had seen the difference it could make in people's lives. Among the recipients of our efforts was the Tewksbury Hospital Equestrian Farm. T.H.E. Farm works with people with both physical and mental disorders, and is situated on state-owned land. Mitt signed a ninety-nine-year lease for it, making certain it would be helping people for almost another century.

Beth Myers first met Mitt when she worked on his 1994 Senate campaign, but we really got to know her in 2002, when she agreed to play his debate sparring partner. As she says, "My first real interaction with Mitt was saying nasty things to him. I was playing his opponent, and I'd answer the question then throw a nasty zinger his way." Beth did such an effective job helping him prepare for the debates that after the election he asked her to become his chief of staff. Later she ran his first presidential campaign. She remained one of his closest advisers. They worked together so well that Beth became known in the media as Mitt's "office wife."

Beth took the job on the condition that she could leave the office and spend the hours between five in the evening and nine in the morning every day with her kids. She had a phone on her desk, and her rule was that if one of her kids called, she answered it. It didn't matter who was in her office, if one of the kids was calling, that took precedence. Only once did Mitt ever say anything about it. Beth's son Curt was very busy being a boy, doing boy things and getting caught at them. He generated a lot of phone calls from teachers and camp counselors. One afternoon, Beth was in an important staff meeting with Mitt and several others when Natalie walked in and told her that Curt's summer camp counselor was on the phone—again. Mitt looked at Beth and said, "Unless Curt has burned down the camp, can he just wait?"

As chief of staff, Beth was at the center of every decision. Her job, as she once described it, was "to put all of the information on the table. Then let Mitt wallow in the data!" Among two of the biggest issues they dealt with were solving the state's fiscal problems and finding a way to get every citizen health insurance. When Mitt took office the state was looking at a multi-billion-dollar budget gap. He managed to balance the budget all four years of his administration, and when he left office, there was a two-billion-dollar "rainy day" fund in the bank.

Crafting a program that would provide access to good health insurance for every citizen and then getting it passed through the legislature would be even more difficult than balancing the state budget. I think that in some ways, my battle with MS was one of the things that led Mitt to take on the challenge. We knew that our own excellent health insurance meant that we could follow whatever medical path we chose to diagnose and treat my disease. But Mitt also knew from his years of service as a lay pastor in our church that people without insurance didn't have the kind of choices we had. In some cases, he saw that people simply couldn't get the care they needed.

Early during Mitt's term as governor, Tom Stemberg, a friend of ours who also happened to be the founder of Staples, the office superstore, stopped by Mitt's office to make a suggestion. He said, "Mitt, why did you run for governor?" Mitt answered as Tom knew he would, "Because I want to help people." Tom then continued: "Well, if you really want to help people, you should find a way to get every citizen health insurance."

Mitt objected, arguing that with the state's finances in such bad shape, there was no way the state would be able to afford to do it. But Tom persisted: "You're smart, Mitt. I'm sure you can find a way."

Mitt and I talked at length about Tom's visit. Mitt also spoke with Beth Myers and other key members of his administration about it. He was certain that there was no way it could be accomplished financially. At the same time, it was a challenge and an opportunity he simply would not brush aside. It was a burr under the saddle.

Months later, Mitt came up with the framework of a plan. Massachusetts was already spending millions of dollars every year to reimburse hospitals that had provided free charity care for people who didn't have health insurance. Those funds came both from the federal government and from state tax revenues. Mitt's idea was to see whether those hospital reimbursement funds could be redirected to help poor uninsured people buy private health insurance. The big question was whether the cost of health insurance would be greater than the reimbursement funds.

Months of analysis and brilliant work led by his secretary of health and human services, Tim Murphy, provided the answer he had hoped for. Not only would the funds be adequate, but they would be more than adequate. The state might actually save money by helping people get insurance rather than having them show up at emergency rooms to get free care that would later be reimbursed by the state.

Mitt's advisers cautioned him that his plan might not sit well with some in his party: health care was seen as a Democratic issue, and anything that sounded like universal health care could make people think of socialized medicine. But Mitt was unmoved. He and his team had worked with the Heritage Foundation, the conservative think tank, and that organization had liked what he came up with. Also, former Republican House Speaker Newt Gingrich had once suggested a similar approach. Requiring people to have health insurance rather than having them expect to get free care paid for by the government was a conservative approach, not a liberal one.

Getting his plan approved by the Massachusetts legislature and also by the federal government presented further challenges. Mitt enlisted his former opponent Senator Ted Kennedy to help with both. He knew that Democratic legislators in Massachusetts would not want to act on health care if Ted Kennedy were opposed. Further, while the people in the Bush administration in Washington were Republicans, they, too, would want to know if Kennedy was going to fight Mitt's idea.

Mitt met several times with Ted. Remarkably, both men put politics aside to find common ground for the common good. The Bush administration also signed on. The Massachusetts legislature took almost a year to put its own stamp on the program, adding several provisions Mitt opposed and which he vetoed. But his vetoes were overridden. In the final analysis, he decided to sign what he thought was 80 percent good and 20 percent not good.

At the signing ceremony in April 2006, held at the historic Faneuil Hall in Boston, Mitt reminded the audience that this was the same place where he had debated Ted Kennedy in 1994. He quipped, "The last time I was on the stage with Senator Kennedy"—he was interrupted by laughter, but continued—"well, this for me feels a little bit like the *Titanic* returning to visit the iceberg." Ted Kennedy had the best line: "Whenever Mitt Romney and Ted Kennedy are celebrating the same piece of legislation, it proves one thing: one of them didn't read it!" The hall erupted in laughter, as did Mitt.

A year or so later, as Mitt began looking at a run for the presidency, he was asked by *Washington Post* columnist Dan Balz whether the Massachusetts health care program, now being referred to as Romneycare, was something he would enact for the entire nation. Mitt explained that, no, it was designed for Massachusetts and probably would not be feasible in other states that had much larger uninsured populations. And Massachusetts already had the most expensive health insurance in the country; imposing it elsewhere could mean skyrocketing premiums in those other states. He felt that the better approach was to require other states to find their own path to get health care for their uninsured.

Being honest, I'd have to admit that Romneycare was a political burden for Mitt's presidential campaigns, particularly after President Obama copied parts of it for his Obamacare legislation. But Mitt never wavered in his conviction that he had done the right thing for the people of his state. By 2012, 97 percent of working-age adults had health insurance, and 99.8 percent of children in the state of Massachusetts were covered. One day, he and I were grocery shopping at the Star Market near our home when a man approached Mitt, shook his hand, and said, "Your health care plan saved my life. Thank you." That wasn't the first or the last time Mitt heard people say that or similar things. So, yes, Mitt is proud of what he, Tim Murphy, Beth Myers, and the entire team accomplished.

I take no credit for Romneycare, but I'm glad that I was part of Mitt's motivation and determination to create and implement it. Perhaps my MS experience had a small but real influence.

I maintained a low profile throughout Mitt's administration. My main task, as it always had been, was to be his partner in living a well-rounded life. Even though I was feeling well, there are certain things that I knew did not mix well with MS. I couldn't stay up late; I needed to get sufficient sleep every night. By ten o'clock I needed to be home. I also had trouble in big, noisy crowds; my senses sometimes became overwhelmed, and I would get dizzy. So, as much as possible, I avoided the banquets and events that are usually part of the life of an elected official's wife. I am also sensitive to certain forms of light; I can't stay too long in fluorescent lighting. But I did use my bully pulpit to bring attention to those things about which I felt strongly, especially teenage pregnancy.

I had been active in several charities for years, including the United Way. I had a particular interest in working with at-risk young women. Over and over I had seen the dreams of teenage girls end when they got pregnant, so I worked to educate them about the consequences of having children before they'd finished their education or established a stable home. I was a volunteer teacher at Mother Caroline Academy, a tuition-free multicultural school for girls between the fourth and eighth grade. One day I asked a fifth-grade class how many of them wanted to go to college. I was thrilled when almost every hand went up. But then I asked how many of them were planning on having a baby before they graduated from high school, and I was devastated when once again almost every hand went up. I told them the truth: they would not be able to do both. They had to make a choice, and that choice would affect everything that happened to them for the rest of their lives.

One thing that I insisted on continuing during Mitt's term as governor was riding horses. I had become physically and emotionally dependent on riding, and if I went more than a week or so without doing so, I felt it. While I would go out to Jan's ranch in California from time to time, I also began working with a dressage trainer in Boston, Maria Harrington. She broke down everything I had already learned and put it back together, helping me understand what it meant to establish a true connection with my horse. My horse, Baron, had become a best friend, companion, and, most important in this sport, teammate.

I began riding in competition. Poor Mitt and our boys were baffled by my love for the sport. I know Mitt kept wondering, maybe hoping, that I would reach the top, that I would win a gold medal in Grand Prix, the sport's top level, so I could be done with it. I explained to him that I was never going to be that good; I would never reach that point. Then he wondered why I would keep working at it. But because it was so important to me, it became important to him. He and the boys would diligently come to the shows and sit there cheering for me as if they had some idea what was going on. But I knew they were rolling their eyes and sneaking peeks at their watches trying to figure out how much longer they'd have to be there. While they couldn't understand exactly what I was trying to accomplish, or why I loved it so much, they were supportive. "You just go around the ring," Mitt said. "Isn't it boring for you?"

I told him, "You have no idea how exciting it is to me." He definitely agreed with me about that. Mitt eventually learned enough about the sport to understand the scoring. He likes to claim that, compared to most other people, he's an expert in it—then he points out that most other people don't know anything at all about it.

I continued to improve. I eventually began posting competitive scores in Grand Prix. In 2006, I was the New England Dressage Association Adult Amateur Champion and I earned gold and silver medals from the U.S. Dressage Federation.

Along with that success came some criticism. There were people in the media who treated this as a rich woman's hobby, rather than appreciating that it was vital for my well-being. Some of the things they wrote were totally inaccurate. One article claimed that I was buying and selling horses for profit. Another speculated that my riding was a fancy tax shelter. Someone else reported that I had won a gold medal for the United States—well, that article I did like. At first, admittedly, all this bothered me. As with so much other reporting, it was frustrating to read stories that simply weren't accurate. But I learned not to pay attention to them.

We have a tradition in Massachusetts known as the lone walk. In Boston, the front doors of the State House are opened only on special occasions. One of them, dating back to 1884, is the day a governor leaves office. He takes the lone walk through those doors and walks across the street and into Boston Common, symbolizing his return to the citizenry. Before Mitt and I took that walk together, he completed another tradition from that same era: he left an inscription in the Bible that remains in the governor's office. He wrote, in part, "To help another person is rewarding. To help many thousands of people has been immensely rewarding."

As we walked through those doors and down the steps, we had a pretty good idea what we would do next. Almost since his election, there had been considerable speculation that Mitt would run for president in 2008. We had discussed it. And when we did, I remembered what Lenore Romney had told me when they asked her why she was running against such a popular incumbent: "If not me, who?"

If not Mitt, who? In early December we'd held a family meeting to discuss the possibility and make the decision. A presidential campaign would have a far greater impact on our lives than the gubernatorial campaign had. Truthfully, we all thought the experience would be similar to that campaign, just magnified. Boy, were we wrong. No one who hasn't been involved in a national campaign could possibly imagine what it's like. We thought, *Hey, this would be a lot of fun*. Once again, my family asked if I was confident a campaign would not have a negative effect on my health. And as before, I told the family that I could handle it, whatever "it" turned out to be. Having been through the campaign for governor and survived it, and believing, as we do, that Mitt would make a wonderful president, the family voted to go for it.

If you want to make God laugh, tell him your plans. Without warning, Josh got sick. As he began to get dressed for work one morning, he noticed a weakness in his hands. It was enough to keep him home for the day to see what was the matter. At first, we were terrified it was MS, but as the day progressed, the weakness intensified and spread to his arms and feet. This was something else entirely. By the next morning Josh was having difficulty walking and went with his wife, Jen, to see his doctor, who recommended that Josh be admitted to the hospital immediately.

Once in the hospital, Josh's symptoms continued to get worse until he reached the point where he was unable to get out of bed. One whole side of his body was affected. I couldn't believe this was happening. Josh's condition was getting worse every day, and no one seemed to know what was wrong. Josh had been my strength through all my trials, and now he was struggling. The family vote aside, Mitt told us that if Josh was sick, he wouldn't run.

The doctors took several MRIs and conducted a series of other tests, including running electrical currents through his arms and legs to test his nerve responses. The results were not good; the doctors concluded that Josh was experiencing the effects of Guillain-Barré syndrome. Little is known about it. It attacks without warning, causes paralysis, and can be life-threatening. But with prompt treatment, most cases gradually dissipate over time. The doctors decided that the best course of action would be to administer intravenous immunoglobulins to slow the effects of the paralysis.

When I pray, I never ask for anything; I simply express my gratitude. Even when Mitt was running for office, I never prayed for him to win—I wouldn't assume to know the will of the Lord. Instead, I prayed for things such as the safety of my family, that they be protected. This time was different. The whole family fasted for twenty-four hours. I had nothing to drink or eat for a whole day. Then I got on my knees and offered a prayer that Josh would be healed. This time I felt I could ask for a favor: "I cannot face having Josh be sick," I said. "He needs to be well. Mitt and I both really need him. If we're going to do this election, we can't do it without Josh." And as I said my prayer, the most peaceful feeling came over me. I felt like I was relaxed.

At just about that same time, doctors and nurses were prepping Josh for his treatment. By this time, Josh was unable to sit up on his own or walk. Before administering the drug, the doctors tested his strength one final time by asking Josh to squeeze his finger as tightly as he could. Josh was unable to even make a fist. The nurse proceeded to insert a port in Josh's arm to administer the drug and almost immediately after she did, Josh felt a surge running through his body. He sat up in bed, much to the astonishment of those in the room. "Excuse me," he told the nurse. "I know you're not going to believe this, but something just happened and I don't think I will be needing the medication." The doctor was called back in and he repeated the strength test he had done earlier; Josh squeezed his finger this time with relatively normal strength. The nurse who had been caring for Josh became very emotional. While she didn't share the same religious beliefs as us, she insisted that she had just seen a miracle from God.

There is no real explanation for what happened with

Josh. He wasn't immediately cured, and it took some time for him to regain all of the feeling in his body. Over a period of several months, he slowly regained his strength and was able to fully support Mitt in the following year with his campaign.

We exhaled. Although Mitt had already filed the necessary forms to run for the Republican nomination, we waited a little more than a month after leaving the State House before he formally announced he was running. He chose to do it in the Henry Ford Museum in Dearborn, Michigan. Appropriately, in the background was a Rambler, the compact car that George Romney had created that revolutionized the auto industry—and just about our entire family. I wasn't the slightest bit nervous when I introduced him. I don't get nervous when I'm completely confident about what I'm saying.

It was an exciting event, and we were all getting ready for the primary campaign. Natalie Crate had been with us in Michigan for the announcement and then went back to Boston. There was a lot of work to be done transitioning to the new governor, Deval Patrick. Natalie was completely involved in that work as well as in helping put together our campaign staff. During the campaign, she was going to be my assistant. Then, one day, in the middle of the night, she had a seizure, and lost the use of one arm. She went into the hospital and they began conducting a series of tests. She called me the next morning wondering if it might be the onset of MS. "Oh, my gosh," I said. "That would be tragic and too ironic."

Obviously we were all very concerned, but we managed

to convince ourselves that it couldn't be anything serious. Her symptoms sounded somewhat similar to Josh's. I had survived a serious disease, Josh was surviving, and so would Natalie. Whatever it was, we'd find a way to take care of her. She was a young woman, she had given birth to her daughter only a few months earlier, she was smart and vivacious, and she was going to accomplish great things both in her career and as a mother. We had access to the best doctors and we had my experience with the system from which to work.

Within a few days we had the test results: Natalie had a stage-three inoperable brain tumor. The doctors said she would live for a year, two at most. The news was beyond devastating. It was tragic. It was so terribly, terribly unfair. She was thirty-four years old and she had a ten-month-old daughter. These things weren't supposed to happen. It made no sense to look for reasons or try to understand why; it just was. It was such a helpless feeling. There was so little we could do. She was in Mass General, one of the great hospitals in the world, but the doctors there were helpless. Mitt and I called pretty much every day. We prayed for her. We tried to find as much information from the research community as we could, hoping there was something new and exciting on the horizon that might make a difference. Maybe there was a new drug being tested, some new theory. We live in an age where medical miracles happen.

There was nothing. Nothing. Natalie was going through the same stages I had been through, but moving quickly from denial and into depression, while her doctors went to work. They were determined to give her every day they could. Her tumor had spread throughout her brain like a spiderweb, so surgery wouldn't help. Instead, she stayed in the hospital and began a regimen of chemotherapy and radiation. For several weeks she refused to see anyone. Believe me, I understood that feeling, and there was nothing anyone could say that would make a difference. A couple of months later, Mitt and I came back to Boston for a fundraiser. To our surprise and delight, we found out Natalie wanted to come to it. That was a big and wonderful surprise. Before the event, we asked her to come up to our hotel room. The drugs made her look a little bloated, and her hair was falling out, but to us she looked absolutely beautiful. She came with her husband and sketched out the details of her disease. She told us the size of the tumor and her prognosis, which was very poor. It was so sobering and sad, so incredibly sad.

Through Natalie, I completed a type of medical cycle. First as an outsider, then a patient, and finally a caregiver. I certainly wasn't her primary caregiver; Natalie had a strong support group; everyone who loved her did his or her part. While I had spoken with many people going through difficult challenges, this was the first time I tried actively to apply the lessons I'd learned to help someone I cared about deeply. The treatment had temporarily beaten back the cancer, but it also had weakened Natalie and made her sick. Having learned the value of adding alternative treatment to Western medicine, I encouraged Natalie to try it. Our positions had been reversed: She had been diligent about helping me deal with my MS. Now I was determined to help her deal with this. At that time I was seeing an acupuncturist. I wanted Natalie to see him. "Look, this isn't going to cure you," I told her. "This isn't going to make the tumor go away, but it might help make you feel better. It might give you a little more energy."

"Oh, Ann, I can't," she said. "I'm too sick to get out of bed."

I took that as a qualified yes. I was determined. "Okay, here's what's going to happen. I'm picking you up, I'm wrapping you in a blanket, and you're going with me. If we just have a nice drive, we'll just have a nice drive. That's fine. But when we get there, if you feel well enough to go inside, we can do that, too. If it works, it works. If it doesn't, it doesn't. It doesn't hurt. Worst case, you and I have a nice visit."

That's what we did. We drove there, and she was able to get out of the car. The acupuncture did appear to help her regain some energy, and she began seeing the acupuncturist for a while. Gradually, Natalie began gaining strength. I would pick her up and take her to some of her appointments, telling her over and over, "Fight, fight, fight." As time passed and the initial wave of depression subsided, she began setting goals for herself. The first one, the one that mattered most, was to live long enough to make sure her daughter had a memory of her mom. Then, as more time passed and she outlived the doctors' predictions, her goal became one day watching her daughter get married.

When Mitt and I were campaigning, we called Natalie regularly. Mitt made sure she stayed on the campaign payroll, as much to remind her how valuable she was to all of us as to help with managing her expenses. There was no pretense. This was just a temporary setback, and eventually she would be able to rejoin the campaign. We all acknowledged exactly what this was: a fight for life.

Three months after Natalie was diagnosed—while we were still absorbing the news—Senator Ted Kennedy was also diagnosed with inoperable brain cancer. Then, incredibly, within a brief period of time, another wonderful young woman, Renee Fry, who had worked in Mitt's administration as director of business and technology and later as deputy chief of staff, had a seizure. Doctors found a brain tumor, as Renee described it, "the size of a racquetball." It just seemed like too much to absorb. At times it made me want to climb back up onto that roof and lie there with my dad looking up at all the stars in the universe and ask him what was going on. Renee's tumor was pushing on her brain, and doctors didn't know if it would affect her sight, her hearing, or her ability to speak. Fortunately, in her case, they were able to operate and remove it—although, eventually, the tumor returned and she had to have a second operation. Her life was saved. What made that situation even more gratifying is that when she received her initial diagnosis, Mitt's term had ended and because she hadn't yet taken another job, she had no health insurance. But under Massachusetts's new state health care plan, she was completely covered. As she happily told Mitt, "Romneycare saved my life." To see what Mitt had worked so hard for make such a difference to someone so close to us was incredibly satisfying.

Natalie . . . Natalie wasn't so fortunate. She fought ferociously, and after a while we fooled ourselves into believing that she had beaten the monster. As she wrote:

As the months passed, my hair grew back, my strength returned even more slowly, and my gratitude ebbed and flowed . . . I had been given more days to hug my baby and kiss my husband, to wake up and look at the towering pines in our backyard while listening to the thunderous roar of the ocean in the distance. I had been granted more summer evenings with my dear family (and beloved dogs) listening to a steamship go by or playing board games, swims in the lake and barbeques with old girlfriends. So how could I possibly forget that I have been granted precious time to live and do what I love? To put it all too simply, life got in the way, cluttering the path with nonsense and clouding my vision with busyness . . .

Starting today, January 2nd [2011] I will be grateful for every day that I open my eyes and breathe deeply. That does not necessarily mean that every single moment will be blissful, exciting or pain-free (as my daughter reminded me frequently over this past weekend). But I will be grateful for the fullness of experience. After all, I'm alive and healthy and once upon a time that was all I ever wanted.

I had learned years earlier from my mother about the will to live. Five days after my mother, Lois, was baptized, her condition deteriorated quickly. I rushed back from Boston to say good-bye. I sat by her bed and cried, but as was typical of her, she tried to make me feel better. "Ann, don't waste another tear," she said. "Everything's wonderful."

She was in terrible pain, but she refused to let go. My brother Rod asked gently, "Mom, what's holding you back?"

"I need to talk to Dave," she whispered. Dave was Mom's younger brother, thirteen years her junior, and she hadn't spoken with him for years, after he'd had a particularly bitter argument with my father. The two men were very different: my father was the regimented engineer; Dave was laid-back and creative. They had tried to work together and clashed, and Dave had been estranged from the family ever since. We didn't know what to expect when Rod got Dave on the phone.

"Dave?" Mom asked.

"Oh, Lois."

"I just wanted to visit with you," she said.

"I know. I've been so bad. Forgive me, forgive me, please."

Mom's eyes were closed. She said, "I had to hear that."

"I'm so sorry."

"Will you let me go? I can't go until we resolve this."

There was softness in Dave's voice as he realized how connected he was to his sister, even after years of their being separated. "Oh, my gosh, my resentment and our separation is what's holding you back? Oh, Lois, I think you are the best sister in the world."

Those words seemed to liberate her. She winced, she sighed, and finally at peace, she closed her eyes forever.

So, believe me, I knew the importance of the will to live. Natalie had fought to live long enough to watch her daughter become a beautiful young girl. And she did. In early 2014, Natalie's tumor came back, and it was more ferocious than ever. This time there was no medicine, no treatment, that could knock it down. We got a call from her husband, Brad, in June 2014 telling us that she didn't have too much longer to live and we needed to come as soon as possible.

It was one of the saddest visits of my life. Brad was protecting her; he hadn't told her that this was the last stage, but obviously she knew. She was forty-one years old, much too young to suffer like that. Her fight had taken every last bit of her energy. Two years, they'd told her, and she'd lived for seven. She lay in a chair, tired and weak, and barely able to speak. We told stories about the governor's office, and she giggled and laughed and added just a few words. Natalie lived long enough to see her daughter become a young lady. She played tennis with her daughter and traveled with her, went to ballet recitals and loved listening to her daughter singing as she practiced the piano. Most important, she lived long enough for her daughter to have memories of her.

Seven

ANY NOTION WE'D had that a presidential campaign was simply a magnified version of what we'd experienced during the gubernatorial campaign was quickly corrected. The media and the cameras were everywhere, and they were focused on trying to get the million-dollar quote or photo. Every word, every expression, was put under a microscope.

After years of dealing with my condition, I had learned a few guiding principles for keeping myself healthy. Get lots of rest, avoid stress, eat well, and get exercise. A campaign is not restful; it is stressful. Sometimes dinner is from a vending machine, and there is very little time or place to exercise. Wherever I was, whatever I was doing, when I felt the first warning signs of fatigue, I had to slow down and recharge. As much as I wanted to contribute, I wouldn't have done myself, or the campaign, any good by relapsing.

Other than that, I was good to go—so I went to New Hampshire.

Iowa and New Hampshire hold the first contests, so their importance in establishing one's position can't be overstated. And those are the two states in which I really had an opportunity to meet people one on one. For me, that's the best part of a campaign, and it is what I do best. In the other states, you're campaigning on a much larger scale; while you're still meeting people, the races there are much more media driven, and it's harder to get to know folks on a personal level. But Iowa and New Hampshire represent politics in person. The first time you meet someone, it's often in their living room. There may be as many as fifty people in that living room, so there isn't much time to chat, but then you'll meet the same people at another small event and say hello, and the next time you see them, they've got a campaign T-shirt on and some items to be signed for their kids. At the next event, they're helping hand out literature, and over time you chat with them and get to know them on a little more than a handshake basis. Throughout a campaign, this gets multiplied by hundreds of people, who become friends.

Often, I've found, people related to me because of my experience with MS. It simply made them feel more comfortable discussing the real problems their families had to deal with. Their stories unfolded as I got to know them.

We Americans are a strong people, and generally we care about a community that's bigger than just ourselves and our families. But it's impossible to campaign without being reminded that many people struggle and work hard to overcome very essential challenges. Every day, we would meet people who themselves or whose family member had encountered a challenge that seemed overwhelming. Often it was a health issue, but particularly during that campaign, when the economy was so down, people wanted to talk about job issues and financial difficulties. Generally people don't show up for campaign events because everything is going well for them. These were people who had worked hard their whole lives. They'd played by the rules, and still they were facing huge obstacles. And they wanted to know which candidate was going to make their lives better.

These people weren't especially interested in abstract numbers. They didn't care about the unemployment rate. They cared about the fact that they or their friends were unemployed. On this level, people tend not to ask questions about policy. Instead, they explain that their unemployment payments were about to run out and they didn't know how they were going to be able to make their next mortgage payment. I was reminded every day that we all are carrying that big heavy bag of rocks on our backs.

This is really the grassroots part of a national campaign. Long before you get to large rallies and begin travelling from place to place by airplane, it's just a few people in a car, often watching the sun rise on the highway to the next town. In 2008, for example, I was in a car with three other women on a freezing cold day in the middle of an Iowa blizzard. We were just about the only car on the road. We were laughing, wondering how we had managed to end up in a snowstorm in Iowa. Suddenly our car skidded on ice and spun several times before sliding into a snowbank.

Thankfully no one was hurt, and we just sat there for a few moments fully appreciating the absurdity of the moment. We dug ourselves out and started up again, and then, to add to it, out of the snowstorm an Amish man driving a horse-drawn buggy trotted by. It was an amazing sight at that time, in that place, in the middle of a snowstorm. That man was completely exposed to the storm, but he didn't seem to mind. Mind? He didn't even seem to notice. "Follow that buggy!" I said. The girls looked at me strangely, and I repeated, "I'm serious. Follow that buggy!" We tracked him to a convenience store/gas station. His horse was parked outside, near the pumps. I went into the store and introduced myself, and then said, "We're in a car and we're freezing. You're in a horse and buggy. How cold are you?" He laughed and sort of shrugged it off: "When the wife and kids need milk, you go get milk."

At the beginning of the 2008 campaign we didn't know how much I could do or for how long. Mitt and I are both better when we're together, so we tried to spend as much time with each other as possible. I found out pretty quickly that campaigning with him probably wasn't the best thing for me. In those early days, Mitt needed to spend a lot of time in small, brightly lit, often noisy rooms meeting and greeting. That was exactly the wrong environment for me, so the campaign eased up a bit on my schedule.

By nature, I'm quite shy. Growing up, I was always the shyest girl in my class. In elementary school, for example, I was the girl they sat between the two noisy boys because the teacher knew there would be no communication through me. I'm most comfortable being in the back of the room talking to one person. But during the campaign, with each day, with each group I met and each hand I shook, my confidence grew. Fortunately, I care about people. Maybe it's possible to fake that. The great comedian George Burns once said that the most important thing in life is sincerity—and if you can fake that you'll do fine. But it has been my experience that people know when you mean what you say. I believed with all my heart what I was telling people: that my husband, Mitt Romney, was the best man to become the President of the United States. I found I was able to relate to people both on a one-on-one basis and in front of a group.

My biggest contribution in 2008 was to be the Mitt Stabilizer. A presidential primary campaign is difficult, and it was new terrain for us. In the end, Mitt finished second in both the Iowa and New Hampshire contests, which was disappointing. He is very competitive, and a big loss can get him down. Behind closed doors, he shows it. (Me, too, by the way.) But my job, as campaign manager Beth Myers told me, "was to pull him out of a bad place." So as often as possible, the campaign would get us together for at least a few hours. It always seemed to work.

Although Mitt won a smaller primary in Wyoming, the next big primary was in Michigan. That was a win-or-forget-it primary for us, because in some ways Mitt was perceived to be a Michigan favorite son. But Mike Huckabee and John McCain were contesting the state, knowing that getting Mitt out of the race would make their own prospects that much easier.

We went on to win the Michigan primary, reigniting

Mitt's prospects. But Michigan meant more than just politics to us: It was the place where we had both been born and raised, and it was the state where Mitt's mom and dad had given so much of themselves. Winning in Michigan felt very, very good.

Every campaign day was a learning experience for the family. Our five boys were touring Michigan in an RV when I responded to a reporter's question that my son Josh would be visiting all ninety-nine Iowa counties in that RV. I can close my eyes and see the look on Josh's face when he heard me say that. It was news to him, too. But Josh did it with his family of five. He had a map on the back end of that RV and as he reached a new county, he'd check it off with a huge marker.

I was continually learning about the media. Through the governor's race, I had sort of figured out how the media worked, and I tried hard not to give them an opportunity to whack me. Overall I think throughout both presidential runs, the media generally was fair to me. I knew they had a job to do and editors to please, and I tried to be friendly and gracious and smiled even when I didn't quite feel like it. As a result, I escaped almost unscathed—almost. Our family's wealth was always an issue in the media and, in many cases, for our opponents. The image that often was conveyed was that we were so wealthy we were out of touch with the average American. Mitt's fifteen years as pastor of church congregations and his service as governor in providing health care for all Bay Staters was simply ignored. I thought it was a terribly unfair portrayal, but once it got ingrained in the narrative, the media ran with it. During a debate in Des Moines, for example, Mitt was asked about his tax policy, and he said, as he believed, "I don't lose sleep thinking about the upper-class tax burden."

According to *GQ* magazine, one of the reporters covering the debate tapped the author of the article on the shoulder and said, "Yeah, he has people on his payroll to do that for him."

I just had to accept criticism without responding. Politics is tough, and it can get ugly. And at times it can get absurd: Even Mitt's teeth got criticized. One unnamed former White House staffer told a reporter that our problem was Mitt was too good looking: "Perfect family, perfect teeth and hair," he said. "The reaction is 'He doesn't understand people like me.'"

I certainly learned a lot during that first presidential campaign. In retrospect, I think I took too much of the criticism personally, which is both counterproductive and destructive. I understood that every candidate's wife was fair game, but admittedly, at times, I did let it get to me. I also allowed myself to get more fatigued than I should have, and by the time the campaign was over, I truly was exhausted, and concerned that I'd left an opening for my MS to sneak back through.

Super Tuesday, the day on which numerous primaries are held and the outcome of the race can pretty much be determined, took place three weeks after our win in Michigan. Twenty-four states and American Samoa held either primary elections or caucuses for Republicans to choose delegates to send to the national conventions. While Mitt won seven states and 201 delegates, John McCain was the big victor, winning nine states and 602 delegates.

Losing that contest was much more difficult than losing to Ted Kennedy more than a decade earlier. That had been an uphill battle, and few people believed that Mitt had a real chance, but we thought we had a very good prospect to win the presidential nomination. After Super Tuesday, Mitt could have stayed in the race, and statistically there was a chance he could have won. Yet, realistically, it was a very long shot, and it would have been destructive to Senator McCain's general election prospects. In order to give the Republican nominee the best chance to win the national election, Mitt decided to drop out. Josh tried to lighten our mood a little, suggesting that there were downsides to winning. But at that moment, in all honesty, I couldn't figure out what they might be.

A part of me was happy it was over—not the way it ended, but that it was over. During a press conference, we were asked if we would consider making another attempt in four years. I looked at Mitt, and it was clear we were on the same page: "Never again." And as I had when I said pretty much the same thing after we lost the election to Ted Kennedy, I meant it. I just couldn't see going through that effort again. None of us could.

It was hard for us to tell how big an issue our Mormon faith would be in the race. It seemed like the press raised the topic in almost every interview. More than four decades earlier, John Kennedy had confronted head-on the invisible barrier to becoming the first Catholic president, and won the election, shattering that barrier forever. But there remained some question about how Americans would feel about a Mormon president. There were polls that indicated that a number of people would not vote for Mitt because of his religion. As we were well aware, the only thing many Americans knew about Mormonism was that at one time polygamy was permitted, although the Church has long prohibited it. During the campaign I actually made a little joke about it, pointing out the irony that at that point in the campaign, Mitt was the only candidate who'd had only one wife.

While it shouldn't have a role in any election, in December 2007 Mitt decided to face it just as Kennedy had done. He made his "Faith in America" speech at the George Bush Presidential Library and Museum in College Station, Texas, explaining, "I do not define my candidacy by my religion. A person should not be elected because of his faith nor should he be rejected because of his faith . . . If I am fortunate to become your president, I will serve no one religion, no one group, no one cause, and no one interest. A president must serve only the common cause of the people of the United States."

My horses made it easier for me to get through the 2008 presidential campaign. No matter what I was feeling, when I was riding I could tune it out and focus on the moment: *Find the right seat. Relax. Balance your weight.* As it had in the past, riding made a difference. I rode all the way through the 2008 election. I didn't spend any time at all thinking about what might have been. Then, in early December, I went for a regularly scheduled annual mammogram at Brigham and Women's Hospital, and was stunned when something showed up on the X-ray. I was diagnosed with ductal carcinoma in situ (DCIS). I didn't know what that meant, either. In fact, it's somewhere between pre-cancer and early-stage cancer. But if it isn't discovered, if you let it go, it can be fatal. Mine was detected so early that it was considered stage 0, the best of all possible stages. I immediately had a lumpectomy, a procedure that went smoothly.

It was a sobering time. First MS, and now this. Either my bag of rocks was getting heavier, or the hill was getting steeper.

After the lump was removed, my doctors recommended radiation. It was interesting. I hadn't worried too much about the cancer. I knew it had been caught early, and I thought, *Well, I'll have surgery and we'll go from there. I'm not going to worry about it until I need to worry about it.* But the prospect of radiation made me very anxious. My father had suffered from prostate cancer for which he had received radiation—and it was that treatment that caused the rare side effect, angiosarcoma, that eventually killed him.

I called my brother Jim, the doctor, to discuss it with him. Having watched my father die from the radiation side effect, I was reluctant to risk following the same path.

Jim told me, "Look, what happened to Dad was so rare."

I said, "I know, but I am clearly his daughter."

"I think you should go ahead with it," he said, maybe a little firmly, as a brother would do.

A lesser concern, but more likely, was that the radiation

Dancing with Tagg and Jen at their wedding reception in July 1992

Margo Gogan and me about to swim with our horses (Utah, 2001)

Screen grab from NBC news coverage of me running with the Olympic Torch. One of the great moments of my recovery—and of my life.

All smiles at the Torino Olympics 2006

With Brad and Natalie Crate, on their wedding day

Announcement day for the 2012 campaign (June 2, 2011, at the Scammans' Bittersweet Farm, Stratham, New Hampshire)

On the campaign trail (2012)

Playing flag football with the campaign staff and traveling press corps before the third and final presidential debate (Boca Raton, Florida, October 22, 2012)

Speaking at the 2012 Republican Convention (Tampa, Florida, August 28, 2012)

In this together. On the campaign trail. (2012)

Chemotherapy takes special strength. On the campaign trail. (2012)

In the green room after the third and final presidential debate, with Beth Myers and Jen Romney (Lynn University in Boca Raton, Florida, October 22, 2012)

The whole family gathers at Lake Winnipesaukee for the annual Christmas Card picture. (August 2014)

Joint birthday celebration with way too many goofy grandsons and granddaughter, Mia (Wolfeboro, New Hampshire)

Reading with Nick, Mia, Grace, and Parker (Wolfeboro, New Hampshire)

Christmas morning wake-up call (La Jolla, 2013)

Mitt, me, and the grandkids jumping into the Grand Canyon waters during the "grandkids trip" (Havasupai reservation, July 2014)

"Grandkids trip" hiking (Zion National Park, July 2014)

Bentley, a powerful horse who helped me make significant progress with the effects of MS

Opening night of the Ann Romney Center for Neurologic Diseases. *Left to right:* Dr. Howard Weiner, Dr. Betsy Nabel, me, Mitt, and Dr. Dennis Selkoe. (Boston, October 2014)

In the research lab at Brigham and Women's Hospital with my doctor, Dr. Howard Weiner, and Dr. Dennis Selkoe

Dancing with my sweetie

might affect my MS. Radiation has been shown to attack the immune system, although not nearly as severely as chemotherapy. No one was really sure whether it might trigger an attack. Radiation also causes fatigue, as your body wages an internal war. But I followed my brother's advice and had the therapy. They blasted my cells. And as I guessed would happen, it knocked me off my feet—literally and figuratively. *Oh shoot*, I thought. *Here we go again.*

I was getting awfully tired of being tired. But this time, at least, I had a strategy that I knew worked. I didn't have to reinvent the wheel; the old one still worked fine. I knew what made me feel better and I knew what made my condition worse. Still, the fatigue would last more than six months before I got my health on balance again.

Among the many people who offered support was the newly elected president, Barack Obama, who called to wish me well. It was a gracious and welcome call.

Each experience, whether it was my health, that of a friend or associate, or one of the many people I met during a campaign, only reinforced what I had learned: there is so much we know about protecting our health, so many things that we now know are good or bad for us, so many different types of precautions we can take and examinations available, that it is not just silly but dangerous not to take advantage of them. Get a mammogram. Get enough sleep. Eat healthy foods. But there also is so much we don't know about protecting our health that it makes great sense to open yourself to the nontraditional options. There was a time I easily dismissed holistic medicine and the alternative therapies that, since I was first diagnosed, have become part of my recovery and part of my life. Nobody really knows what therapy will work for an individual or, if or when it does, why it works. The fact that it does is enough. For me, reflexology, yoga, acupuncture, meditation, horses, and faith, as well as a healthy diet consisting of organic foods and little meat—with a healthy dose of vitamin D from sunlight—have made all the difference. It's a jumble that resulted from trial and error. I've tried therapies that worked for people I knew but did not seem to make a difference for me. Who knows why, and honestly it makes no difference. Western medicine had stopped the progression of MS, it helped me battle cancer, but I had learned other strategies to help with my energy; I had found my balance. That balance was precarious, and I knew that I was still vulnerable.

Within a year following the 2008 election my health was good and life was good. As soon as an incoming president raises his right hand and takes the oath of office, the clock begins ticking on his four-year term—and the speculation begins about the next election. It isn't simply idle talk: gearing up to run is a long and very expensive process. Millions of dollars have to be raised. A lot of people have to be hired to build and run a campaign. If you wait too long, it becomes impossible. There also are a lot of very good people busy trying to hitch a ride on what they believe will be the winning campaign. Only a few weeks after the 2008 election, Mitt began receiving feelers from people trying to discern his interest in making another run. Many people perceived him to be a very strong contender for the nomination.

But there were a lot of alternatives for us. Almost immediately after dropping out of the 2008 race, Mitt also began receiving offers to get back into the business world. One of them was an offer to run a hedge fund with an annual salary of twenty million dollars. He turned them all down. Somewhere deep inside, I knew what that meant. When it's an important cause where Mitt thinks he can make a difference, he does not walk away easily—and when he does lose, he doesn't like to walk away.

Mitt and I rarely spoke of making another run for the presidency. We make decisions together, we have to talk through everything, but this topic we let sit there. It wasn't until it was time to make a go or no-go decision that we talked through how we felt. We considered all the positives and all the negatives. We knew all the risks. Did I believe he would make a good president? Yes. So the answer to running again, despite that I had said "never again," was yes. Mitt, however, needed a push to get to the same place.

In December 2010, the family gathered to discuss whether Mitt should make another run for president. Surprisingly, there was no mention of all the time and work each of us had put into the last campaign, though I'm sure Josh had not forgotten his ninety-nine-county RV journey through Iowa. We talked about the high points: the surprising come-from-behind win in Michigan, the scores of new friends we had made among supporters and donors, the political and other leaders we had come to know. We also were honest about the low points: Florida's Charlie Crist going back on his word, the loss in New Hampshire, and the less-than-adoring press. The political environment had changed since 2008. President Obama's administration had led some Republicans to be more strident, even angry, in their opposition to the direction the country was heading in. One former governor said that while he had considered running for president in 2012, he felt that the primary electorate had become so toxic that he would not be a fit with our voters.

Mitt pointed out that if he were to run again, he would have to carry the baggage that had been placed on him by Senator McCain's 2008 primary campaign, joking that he had been branded as a "flip-flopping Mormon." He also noted that removing an incumbent president is a rare and difficult thing to do. Yes, he said, the economy was a problem for President Obama, but because many people placed the blame for the great recession on President Bush, it did not impact Obama's reelection prospects as much as would have been expected. Noting that every recession ends and that every recovery reduces unemployment, he predicted that if the rate of unemployment stayed above 8 percent, the president would lose, but if it dropped below that level, Obama would probably be reelected. Beating President Obama would, to a significant degree, be out of our control.

There was also the primary to consider. The primary opponents would blame Mitt for showing President Obama the path from Romneycare to Obamacare. And good people were looking seriously at the race: Governor Tim Pawlenty was a capable and accomplished leader, Newt Gingrich had been Speaker of the House, Governor Rick

Perry had overseen impressive economic growth in Texas, and while they would eventually decide not to run, Mitch Daniels, Chris Christie, Mike Huckabee, and Haley Barbour were all thinking about a run.

With all this in mind, we put it to a vote. The 2006 family vote had been unanimous in favor of running. This time the vote was 10–2 against. Only Tagg and I voted in favor. Even Mitt voted against, wondering, "Why go through the process just to lose again?"

All his preparatory work had convinced him that it would be incredibly difficult to defeat an extremely well-funded incumbent president, even if he did win the nomination. But in addition to Tagg and me, a lot of other people kept pushing him to change his mind. This wasn't a matter of Mitt being coy, as some journalists suggested; he was being logical, realistic. His career in business had shown him the downside of making ego-driven decisions. He didn't need to make this run to prove anything to anyone.

Over the coming weeks, Mitt came around to my way of thinking. There were several things that led him to his decision. First, he was increasingly concerned about the direction the country was taking under President Obama. Internationally, Mitt felt that President Obama had seriously underestimated the intentions of Russian president Vladimir Putin, minimized the reality of the growing threat of radical Islam, distanced America from our most loyal friends, and was walking away from Iraq and Afghanistan in a way that would ultimately result in chaos and bloodshed. At home, he felt that the president had done nothing to make American businesses better able to create the jobs that would raise incomes and provide opportunity for the middle class.

Mitt had also come to believe that among those considering a run in 2012, he would have the best chance of beating the president in the general election. Winning the nomination, however, he knew would not be a foregone conclusion. As his strategist Stuart Stevens observed, Mitt was Mormon in a party that was more evangelical; he was rich in a party that was more populist; and he was northern in a party that was more southern. Added to that was Romneycare.

In the final analysis, Mitt and I agreed: get in and give it our all.

This time, Mitt had the national campaign experience he lacked in the 2008 race. He reviewed the lessons learned from his loss to Senator McCain and from the senator's loss to Barack Obama. He assembled a cadre of some of the nation's prominent authorities on foreign and domestic policy and tasked them with preparing thorough briefings. He assembled a campaign team that not only was expert but comprised people of character and caring. Win or lose, these people would be the kind who would remain friends—his friends and friends with one another.

His prior experience was not all positive, however. In the 2008 primaries, his opponents branded him a flip-flopper, an epithet the media was happy to keep alive. Our wealth and Mitt's career as a private equity CEO would also be dragged out, to foster the continuing narrative that he didn't care about everyday people. Nothing was further from the truth, of course. It was his concern for the everyday people of America that had led him to decide to run for president. And it was the warmth of his heart that we had seen in our home, that members of his church had seen in the congregations he pastored, and that his colleagues had seen in the places he had worked. It could not have been lost on the people who follow campaigns closely that Mitt was being vigorously supported by the people who knew and had known him best.

Before the campaign got under way, we made decisions about my participation. We agreed that I would spend two or three days a week campaigning, and then take time off. I would do some light interviews whenever possible, but as I reminded everyone, I couldn't work as hard as Mitt. This came as no surprise: not a lot of people work as hard as Mitt. When necessary, I once again would become the Mitt Stabilizer. While most of the time Mitt and I campaigned separately, at least once a day the campaign tried to get us together by phone, even if only for a few minutes. I did sit in on a lot of strategy sessions, where my main function was to be Mitt's sounding board. We'd spent our lifetime together discussing every important issue that affected our family, and this was no different. It was just a little bigger family.

This time the things that had gone wrong in 2008 went right for us. As we approached Super Tuesday, it looked like we were going to win the nomination. My competitive nature kicked in, I got caught up in the excitement and enthusiasm, and I overdid it. I couldn't quit, and I didn't want to tell anyone how tired I was. But I started to reach that point where I begin to lose my words—when I'm that fatigued,

I can't find the words to express what I'm thinking. Then I started to stumble a little bit, losing my balance when I shouldn't have. I finally accepted the fact that I had to take a break.

In fact, two weeks later, after we won the Illinois primary, I had to take ten days off, spending as much of that time as possible on horseback. While the emotional distance between my normal life and my life in the barn had always been significant, it really was nothing compared to what we were going through. On the campaign trail, every moment of our lives was planned, every single minute counted. Every word carried great weight, and even the smallest mistake could prove consequential. It was the greatest game of gotcha anyone could possibly imagine. It was almost impossible not to make mistakes. Once, for example, when I was asked during a Baltimore radio interview if Mitt came across as too stiff, I responded that if that was true, then "we better unzip him and let the real Mitt Romney out." The communications folks on the campaign didn't think this was the most ideal response.

Later during the campaign, my airplane was forced to make an emergency landing in Colorado after some wiring caught fire and filled the cabin with smoke. It was scary for several moments, but no one was hurt. After our plane was safely on the ground and I'd spoken to Mitt and assured him we all were fine, he told a *Los Angeles Times* pool reporter that smoke in an airplane was especially dangerous because "you can't find any oxygen from outside the aircraft to get in the aircraft, because the windows don't open. I don't know why they don't do that." While the *Times* reporter made it clear that Mitt was very relieved and was joking, other reporters took his comment seriously—and they used it as a basis for questioning Mitt's intelligence. Such is the nature of the sound bite in the hands of a less-than-adoring press.

So, as you can imagine, the contrast between the endless cameras and microphones of the campaign and then being alone, mucking out a stall, grooming an animal, sitting on a horse, being in a quiet and safe environment, was indescribable.

The primaries were as exhausting as we knew they would be, but the outcome was as exhilarating as we had hoped. Mitt received a resounding vote of confidence from Republicans across the country. He would formally accept the nomination of the Republican Party at the Republican National Convention in Tampa in August 2012. And I would be a prime-time speaker.

Mitt was a little concerned about my speaking to an audience of millions. He hadn't seen me very often on the trail, as we generally spoke at our own separate events. But I had spoken to large audiences and had no trouble finding my voice and speaking my mind. So as I stood in front of the convention hall I wasn't in the least bit nervous. That may sound a little unbelievable, but it is true. I was actually looking forward to my speech. This was my chance to tell the American people why Mitt should be president and why he would be a great president. This was also my chance to thank the millions of mothers who were helping raise the next generation of Americans.

In preparing what I would say, I thought back to the

remarks I had made at Harvard Business School decades before. I had noted that being a mother and actively raising a child was every bit as demanding as other important professions, and surely just as rewarding. There had been a lot of changes in the home and workplace since I'd made that speech. A lot more women were trying to find the balance between a career and their children, but there still was a stigma attached to putting your children before your job. In fact, several months earlier a Democratic spokesperson had criticized me on CNN for suggesting that women care about economic issues, saying, "Guess what? His wife has actually never worked a day in her life." Whoa. That comment really surprised me. To suggest that raising children is not work was disappointing to me and, I suspected, to many millions of other American women. But it reminded me of how many people still believed it. I decided I would address the merits of motherhood in my speech.

Let Mitt talk about economics and foreign policy. My speech focused on the thing about which I was an undeniable expert: being a mother. I also wanted it to be a thank-you note to the mothers who had worked so hard and felt so underappreciated. "It's the moms who always have to work a little harder to make everything right," I said. "It's the moms of this nation—single, married, widowed—who really hold this country together. We're the mothers, we're the wives, we're the grandmothers, we're the big sisters, we're the little sisters, we're the daughters . . .

"You're the ones who always have to do a little more.

"You know what it's like to work a little harder during the day to earn the respect you deserve at work and then come home to help with that book report which just has to be done.

"You know what those late-night phone calls with an elderly parent are like and those long weekend drives to see how they're doing.

"You know the fastest route to the local emergency room and which doctors actually answer the phone when you call at night.

"You know what it's like to sit in that graduation ceremony and wonder how it was that so many long days turned into years that went by so quickly . . . Tonight we salute you and sing your praises.

"I'm not sure if men really understand this, but I don't think there's a woman in America who really expects her life to be easy . . .

"And that is where this boy I met at a high school dance comes in. His name is Mitt Romney . . .

"I read somewhere that Mitt and I have a storybook marriage. Well, in the storybooks I read, there were never long, long rainy winter afternoons in a house with five boys screaming at once. And those storybooks never seemed to have chapters called MS or breast cancer. A storybook marriage? No, not at all. What Mitt Romney and I have is a real marriage. I know this good and decent man for what he is—warm and loving and patient . . ."

And . . . we were off.

The memory that we had once believed that a presidential campaign was just a magnified version of a gubernatorial campaign was laughable. I had my own campaign staff—or, as it became known, Ann World. I had the most wonderfully supportive people working with me, and we made a stressful situation as much fun as possible, trying always to find the humor in a very serious situation. We also were fortunate in that the media coverage we got was not as strident as before; it was a little more relaxed and feature-story oriented. Mitt was on the front pages every day; we would have been just as happy to be in the Home section. In Mitt's "bubble," when his staff found themselves with an extra few minutes, they used the time to go over the talking points for his next appearance or deal with campaign strategy. In Ann World we all laughed a lot and had a great time together. The only time we even heard from the campaign was if I said something that maybe I shouldn't have: *Ann, you shouldn't have responded to this remark or that newspaper column.* And on occasion senior members of the campaign would pop into Ann World for a day or two to decompress.

The events we did in Ann World were people-oriented rather than policy-oriented, and as many of those people as possible were women. On Rachael Ray's TV show, for example, we cooked Mitt's favorite meal: mini-meatloaf cakes topped with a sauce spiked with brown sugar. At another kitchen show appearance, I made my well-known Welsh cake cookies, and then, without thinking about it, started stacking the dirty dishes on the TV set. In Jacksonville, Florida, I read a Dr. Seuss book to a kindergarten class and then spoke at a rally of mostly women. When I was asked on *Live! With Kelly and Michael* about my statement after the previous election that we were not ever going to do this again, I told them that Mitt had laughed and responded, "Do you know what? You say the same thing after every pregnancy."

My role in the campaign was pretty straightforward: allow the public to know the private Mitt Romney. When asked during an interview in *Good Housekeeping*, for example, what was the biggest misconception about Mitt, I responded, as I did every day, "He is so warm and approachable, very spontaneous and funny in his private life—which is not what you see in his public life."

We were always on the move. It was a whirlwind of media appearances, rallies, and fund-raisers, countless fund-raisers. And as before, I was touched by the many people struggling with their own issues who identified with me and wanted to meet me. They rarely, if ever, wanted anything more than an opportunity to say hello and to tell me that they were supporting our campaign. My message to them was always the same: Hold on, help is coming. I didn't want to get ahead of myself, but in the back of my mind I had begun thinking about those initiatives I would focus on if we won. Obviously MS and breast cancer research were near the top of my list. Coincidently, Michelle Obama's father also was afflicted with MS, which caused him to spend most of his life walking with two canes. That wasn't going to be my whole platform, but I certainly wasn't going to ignore it. Encouraging research, conversation, and communication about those diseases was going to be a big piece of what I wanted to accomplish.

My disease became an issue only once during the campaign. There were reporters who mocked the fact that a horse I owned was going to be ridden in the London Olympics dressage competition, which was simply another way of attacking Mitt as being out of touch with the average American. One group actually made an ad about it. Another journalist decided that it would be better for our campaign if the horse lost, as it would get too much publicity if the United States won a gold medal. When I was warned years earlier that politics was really tough and everything you did counted, I don't think I suspected it would get down to that level. When it was pointed out to the media that riding was an important therapy for me, the attacks faded away.

When anything like that happened, Mitt immediately wanted to protect me. That was funny, of course, because while he was busy trying to protect me, I was trying to protect him. At the same time that he was calling my staff and telling them not to work me so hard, I was telling his staff not to work him so hard. There were times when we hadn't seen each other for a while, and Mitt got wound up and became frustrated and his staff said, "Okay, it's time for Ann to come back again. Get the Mitt Stabilizer in here." We just worked better as a team. Always have, always will.

But there finally did come a time when everything caught up with me. At a major event in Naples, Florida, I introduced Mitt, went backstage, sat down, and said, "I'm done." I was empty, I couldn't go another step. They put me in a car and drove me across the state, and I spent three days recharging.

There isn't a college course called "running for president." There are very few people who have had the experience, and there isn't much advice they can give you. You just get up every day and do it. And then you do it again, and again. As I was learning, a presidential campaign is the biggest roller-coaster ride in the world. The ups are incredible, and the lows are devastating. If you let yourself go for the ride, within a few hours you can go from exhilaration to depression. We learned pretty quickly not to let any news, good or bad, affect us. Oh, that was hard to do sometimes. Sometimes all the emotion wells up inside and you just want to let it out in a huge burst—and you can't. Well, you shouldn't. On a couple of occasions, I probably said more than the campaign would have liked, and I was criticized for it in the media. Instead, you have to keep smiling.

There were a few times when I did feel it was necessary to speak up. The polls before the first debate with Barack Obama showed we were still behind and didn't seem to be gaining traction. So finally, before the debate, we all sat down to discuss what we hoped Mitt would accomplish in it. I emphasized that Mitt needed to let the American public see that he was a lot more than a collection of policies. We wanted people to see him for who he really was, not for who the Obama campaign and its surrogates had made him out to be.

From the very beginning, the opposition's strategy had been to attack Mitt not for his policies, but for being a rich, out-of-touch plutocrat who didn't care about everyday people. His being a CEO and rich helped their narrative. And perhaps his being Mormon amplified the image that he wasn't like you and me, that he couldn't connect with people. Mitt is the first to admit that he helped this unfortunate narrative along with some of the things he said during the campaign, as when he explained famously that to win he didn't need to get 100 percent of the vote because 47 percent were sure to vote for the opposition. He needed to win the swing voters, he explained. That "47 percent" comment hurt him.

Mitt saw the debates in exactly the same way I did: as an opportunity for people to see that what the opposition had said about him simply was not true. President Obama, for example, had been saying that Mitt would lower taxes for the rich—again, painting him as a plutocrat. Mitt would correct that untruth and argue for tax reduction for the middle class. Most important, he would explain his positions by drawing on personal experiences and by telling the stories of real people he had met during the campaign.

My job during every debate was to be visible to him. The first thing Mitt did when he walked onstage was to find me in the audience. As I stood there, anticipating the first time America would see my Mitt and President Obama face off, I thought about a lot of things. I thought about how lucky we were to have come so far. I thought about how lucky *I* was to have regained my strength, to have my MS in check. About how much love and strength and faith Mitt had given me. About listening to the right rein. About being quiet, and letting God show us the path. About my father, on the roof, and the grand design.

Mitt must have been thinking about a lot, too. I know for one thing he was thinking about *his* father. As he stood at the lectern at that first debate—and as he would do in each debate thereafter—he wrote one word, encircled, at the top of his notes: *Dad.*

And they were off. The first question in that debate was about the economy. Mitt began his response with a story I'd told him: "Ann yesterday was at a rally in Denver, and a woman came up to her with a baby in her arms and said, 'Ann, my husband has had four jobs in three years, part-time jobs. He's lost his most recent job, and we've now just lost our home. Can you help us?' And the answer is yes, we can help, but it's going to take a different path, not the one we've been on, not the one the president describes as a top-down, cut taxes for the rich. That's not what I'm going to do."

For the next hour or so, Mitt was at his best. He was clear, empathetic, sensible, logical—he was all the things that his family, friends, and colleagues knew him to be.

That debate was a high for us. Mitt won it resoundingly, as polls and pundits uniformly attested. It injected a whole new enthusiasm in the campaign, which carried through all the way to Election Day. It was amazing: the more people had seen of him, the larger the crowds became.

The second debate focused on foreign policy, a place where a sitting president has an obvious advantage. President Obama mocked Mitt's assertion that Russia was America's number one geopolitical foe, saying that the eighties were calling and that they wanted their foreign policy back. It was as good a line as it was as bad a reading of Russia, as subsequent events would prove.

Later, there was an exchange between the president and

Mitt about the attack on our ambassador in Libya. The president said he had called the attack "terrorism," and Mitt argued that his administration had tried to characterize it not as terrorism but as the spontaneous reaction to a video shown in Egypt. Shockingly, the moderator, Candy Crowley of CNN, injected herself into the exchange, saying that the president was right. Mitt was nearly speechless.

I don't recall ever seeing Mitt angrier than he was after that debate. He was angry that the moderator had interrupted the exchange. Of course, the administration had done exactly as Mitt had argued: it had claimed for several days that this was not a planned terrorist attack. Mitt was right in principle, as Candy Crowley later confirmed. But he did not look like he was right during the debate itself, particularly given Crowley's intrusion.

Polls after the debate gave the president the win, but by a relatively small margin. It looked like Republicans sided with Mitt, Democrats with the president, and the plurality of Independents with the president as well.

The final debate was perhaps the least memorable. Mitt's personality showed through, however, and it won him even greater enthusiastic support. When Mitt came off the stage, his staff and friends met him in the hallway, clapping and cheering that he had won another great debate. We felt like we were on cloud nine.

During the last few weeks of the campaign, you could feel the enthusiasm and energy growing. One factor in winning an election is to peak enthusiasm as close to Election Day as possible, in order to generate the largest possible turnout. In a country that is so evenly divided politically as the United States is, the election can depend on who gets their voters to the polls.

On Election Day we felt calmly confident. Our internal polls showed the trends moving in our direction in key swing states. Independent voters in Ohio, for instance, were solidly for Mitt. While the campaign carried out extensive planning for a transition, which was traditional and necessary, we didn't talk about it at all. We returned to Boston to await the results.

And then the numbers started coming in. It slowly became clear that we did not get the turnout we had anticipated. The president's ground game was better than ours. There really is no way to describe what we were feeling. I know it is a cliché, and I've read these words often myself and doubted them, but the truth is I felt worse for what America had lost than what we had lost. More than anyone else in the world, I knew the kind of president Mitt would have been.

I suppose there are some people who might suggest that I should not have taken the loss with much difficulty. There was a time a decade earlier when I thought my life was over or that I would be spending the rest of it in a wheelchair. Instead, I was living a full and wonderful life. We were blessed with five sons, five daughters-in-law, eighteen grandchildren, and one more on the way. As had become well known in the campaign, we were financially set. The life we would return to was one full of love and laughter. All that was true, but I knew what had been possible for this country, so I knew what was lost.

I cried.

Other people might remind me that I had my faith for support, which remained unshaken. There is truth to that, but honestly that night it made little difference.

An incredible mix of emotions ran through me: sadness, anger, relief, disbelief, depression, acceptance, and just about anything else you might mention other than happiness. While the returns from Ohio had made the result clear, some members of our campaign staff didn't want to concede. The field teams in Ohio, Virginia, and Florida reported that the races there were still very close and were urging Mitt to ask for recounts. But Mitt shook his head and said, "It's not going to happen."

When Mitt asked his assistant to make the call to the Obama headquarters, I couldn't hold it in any longer and I began crying. When you pour as much of your life and your energy and your passion into an effort and it doesn't turn out the way you hoped, it's unbelievably sad. Crying is the appropriate response in that situation. We were with Paul and Janna Ryan, and Janna cried with me.

Eventually Mitt had to go give his concession speech. Mitt is always at his best in the most difficult times. After thanking all the people who had given so much of themselves for so long, he said, "I also want to thank Ann, the love of my life. She would have been a wonderful First Lady. She has been that and more to me and our family." Boy, standing on that stage, I found it hard not to cry in front of all those cameras.

It had been the most incredible experience imaginable, impossible to describe, really, but it was over. A day later was another sad good-bye when our Secret Service detail hugged each of us, got in their cars, and drove away. They had become a part of our family, and we loved them.

In the coming months, we stayed away from the media as much as possible. A picture of Mitt pumping his own gas was published, as if Mitt had never pumped his own gas before. Another one showed us in a movie theater seeing the film *Twilight*. In other words, we were living our normal life. The adjustment back to normal life is instant, but it takes some time to get used to it again. I went riding as often as possible, but it often wasn't enough. We actually didn't spend any time wondering about the what-ifs: you can spend a lifetime living with regrets if you allow that to happen. The most frustrating part for me is that people didn't get to know Mitt for who he is. To watch him portrayed in a negative light was maybe the hardest thing for me.

It took a couple of months before we got completely back on track. I remember the moment perfectly. It was February 15, 2013. The phone rang at 6:00 A.M. Mary, Craig's wife, was due to give birth so we were anticipating this call. It was Craig and he was elated. "Craig," I said, "what did you have? A boy or a girl?"

Craig and Mary had told us they wanted to surprise us with the sex of their child; even they weren't going to find out until the birth.

"A boy," he said.

Oh darn, I thought. Selfishly, I had been hoping for a girl. We are a family full of males. "That's wonderful," I said.

"And a girl," he added.

That's when I began screaming with joy.

Eight

IN A "LIFE TO-DO LIST" Howard Weiner has compiled over years of seeing patients struggle with neurologic diseases, he emphasizes giving—in dealing with MS in particular, but really to deal with all challenges. Maybe where I was fortunate is that in my family serving others has always been part of our lives. Certainly Mitt has been doing it for decades as part of his participation in our Church and working with charities close to his heart. Our boys have each found a way to give back for what they've received, but the contribution of my brother Jim stands out.

Jim and Becky have seven children of their own, three through birth and four by adoption, but they got involved, seriously involved, when the children of close friends were diagnosed with cystic fibrosis. This is an awful disease in which the victim's lungs eventually get so scarred that they cease to function, causing the victim to suffocate. It's awful. Worse, these children had a secondary, rare and deadly form of something called *Burkholderia cepacia* bacteria, which made treatment even more difficult and complicated.

At nineteen, Justin Sabin, an Eagle Scout who loved to laugh and would have given so much to the world, died at home. Two years later his sixteen-year-old sister, Jennifer, began exhibiting some of the same terrible symptoms. To survive, she was connected to oxygen tanks; she lived with an IV in her arm, lost her appetite, and suffered fevers and nausea. She had so little energy that even brushing her teeth was a monumental task. Every breath she took, she said, was like gasping for air through a straw.

The only hope was a lobar lung transplant, a procedure in which a living donor gives a lobe of his or her lung to the patient, which will eventually replace the damaged lung. The Sabin family didn't qualify as donors, so they needed to find two people who would volunteer to have this difficult and sometimes dangerous surgery. It would require that an incision be made in the donor's back and several ribs be broken to remove the lobe. Complete recovery would take as long as ten months, maybe longer.

More than thirty members of the Sabins' church volunteered, including my brother Jim and a real estate investor named Graham Bullick. (After those two were selected, Jennifer's father quietly offered them an opportunity to change their minds, telling them he could have them eliminated for medical reasons. They said no.) The operation, in which surgeons removed parts of the lungs from the three people involved and implanted the new lobe into Jennifer's body, took more than two hours.

For the next few days, as Jennifer fought for her life, she was connected to supporting medical equipment and more than a dozen tubes and intravenous lines. Eventually she stabilized—and began improving. As she later wrote about the surgery, "Mom and Dad came into the room and Mom asked me how I felt. I took a deep breath, something I hadn't been able to do in a long, long time, and began weeping . . . [C]ystic fibrosis was forever gone from my new lungs, and I was going to live."

Less than three weeks after the operation, my brother Jim was back to work, performing eye surgery.

My turn to make a big contribution came months after the election. Eventually Mitt and I got back to our normal lives. The phone rang often, with various offers for things in which one of us might get involved. One that I considered was being a contestant on *Dancing with the Stars*. That show is among my guilty pleasures. Not only do I watch it, but in early 2013 Craig and I attended the season finale. Coincidently, among the people we met at the studio that night was Montel Williams, who also has MS, and is as big a fan of the show as I am. So I was flattered when producers invited me to participate the following season. But I realized that not only was I not as flexible as I would have needed to be, but it would have required a time and energy commitment I wasn't certain I could fulfill. The last thing I wanted to have to do was start and then drop out if the rehearsals caused a relapse. And when I saw that Dorothy Hamill had been picked to participate, I was glad I'd made the decision; I didn't want to compete against her!

There also was speculation that after Senator Kerry resigned to become secretary of state, I had been asked by the Massachusetts Republican Party to run for his seat. There were people who believed it would be a fun thing for me to do and that I could win. But nobody asked me, and I wondered if anyone had actually stopped to consider if it would have been fun for me. Having been deeply involved in state and national politics, I can say without reservation, there isn't a chance of my ever running for office. There are many things I consider fun; a political campaign is not one of them.

But there was one thing I did say yes to, and it came as a surprise to me, as it was not something I had ever thought about. During the campaign I had been in touch with Dr. Weiner several times. I would call to tell him, "I haven't forgotten. This is going to be my initiative if we win." During one of those conversations, he told me that an Alzheimer's vaccine they were developing had produced some really exciting results in the lab and they were getting ready to test it. An Alzheimer's vaccine? That really caught my attention. That would change millions of lives and save billions of dollars. That's unbelievable, I said. It was my turn to get excited. Maybe we should broaden what we want to do, I suggested. Among those things that I most regretted after the election was what we might have been able to do if we'd won.

When I went to see Dr. Weiner for my annual CLIMB

evaluation, we started talking about "what might have been" wistfully. Then we suddenly thought, why not do it anyway? Why not go ahead? It wouldn't be as big, it probably wouldn't be as effective, but it would be something. The more we discussed it, the more excited I became. We had already broadened our concept to include Alzheimer's, but as we talked, we realized we could do something bigger in neurologic diseases. More than two and a half million people have MS, but when you combine them with the number of people suffering from Alzheimer's and ALS and Parkinson's and brain tumors, suddenly the numbers rise drastically. In fact, as I've learned, neurologic diseases affect more than 50 million people worldwide. In some way, almost every family everywhere is brushed with the consequences of a neurologic disease.

The biggest challenge facing the center was fund-raising. Dr. Weiner estimated that he and Dennis Selkoe had spent as much as 25 percent of their time raising funds to keep the center moving forward. Money buys time and research, he told me. Later Dr. Selkoe told me a story about traveling to Japan with Dr. Weiner in 1990 to try to raise money to further their research. As they walked around the Imperial Palace in Tokyo they talked about the future, and what was possible, and how much money it would take. A lot, they realized, a whole lot. And the only place to get as much as they needed was from American philanthropy. Howard Weiner summed it up best: his exact words were "Research is like crossing the desert. I don't want to go across the desert without enough water." That was one area where I believed I could be helpful.

Most research centers focus on a single issue, but clearly there is a connection between several significant neurologic diseases. As Dr. Weiner explained it, medical research was done in silos, but if we really wanted some quick break-throughs, there would have to be a lot more collaboration. As he and Dr. Selkoe had learned through four decades of friendship and collaboration, the more detectives work-ing the crime scene, the more evidence is going to be uncovered. There is no question that any discovery made about how the brain functions might have application to other conditions. While there was a lot of research being done in various areas, there was little cross-pollination. Bringing together scientists studying several different diseases would greatly increase opportunities for fund-raising. Dr. Weiner and Dr. Selkoe eventually settled on a platform consisting of five diseases that affect the brain: MS, Alzheimer's, Parkinson's, ALS or Lou Gehrig's disease, and brain tumors. Dr. Weiner went through the overlapping relationships among each of these diseases with me, point-ing out, "The mechanisms in one disease exist in the others." Changes in the immune system of a patient with MS, for example, were found in the immune system of pa-tients with ALS. I was surprised by the inclusion of brain tumors, believing, as most people do, that tumors would not have a clear relationship with MS or Alzheimer's. But of course they do. Both MS and brain tumors, Dr. Weiner explained to me, are related to regulatory cells, T-cells. In MS, a lack of regulatory cells provokes the immune system into being overactive; in brain tumors, the tumors somehow cause the immune system to create too many regulatory cells, which eventually overwhelm the immune system. "We hypothesized that if we used a new antibody we found in our MS research to knock down the regulatory cells in tumors," Weiner explained to me, "then the immune system may be more effective and the tumors would shrink." He smiled and added, "And that's actually what we found."

Remembering Natalie Crate, I was thrilled that we would be able to include finding a way to prevent and treat brain tumors as one of our initiatives.

Proving there is overlap among these diseases, Dr. Selkoe told me that his lab recently "made a new discovery in Parkinson's, based on our Alzheimer's work, but that still has much further to go."

Together Dr. Weiner and I began thinking of ways I could be helpful in the effort to create a larger neurologic center. How wonderful it would be to help provide an answer for all those MS patients who approached me asking for advice. While dancing with many stars would have been a lot of fun, this was something I could do that might make a real difference in people's lives. I remembered the terror I felt when I was first diagnosed and read all this scary stuff, and I thought how wonderful it would be if there was one place newly diagnosed patients could go that would provide complete and accurate information, as well as the encouragement they needed, at that most vulnerable time. Among the things I thought we could do was create a community to fill that need—a place that would, among other things, help people understand their symptoms and give them hope. Putting my name on it was never part of my thinking. It's not the type of thing Mitt and I have ever done. But that's what ended up happening.

Tagg's business partner, Spencer Zwick, had served as the finance chairman for Mitt's campaign, and successfully raised almost half a billion dollars. He is a wonderful, giving man, whom we sometimes refer to as our sixth son. He is an expert at raising money for charities. So I asked him to meet with Dr. Weiner to determine the ways in which I could be especially helpful raising funds for the center. Spencer is sensitive to this issue because his own son has a form of MS, so he is quite knowledgeable about the fight. Apparently during their meeting he said, "You know, if we really want to make this big, we should ask Ann to put her name on it."

It says quite a bit about the two doctors, who have devoted their lives to creating this center, that rather than wondering why their names, which rightly belong, aren't on the stationery, they instantly embraced this concept and then enthusiastically began trying to convince me to agree to it. "I'm pretty uncomfortable about that," I responded. "Why don't we go out and look for a really big donor and name it after them." Believe me, I knew the value (to some people) of naming rights. Mitt, too, wasn't especially comfortable with the idea.

But Spencer, more than anyone else, pushed. It'll give us great visibility, he insisted. Howard wanted me to be the center's so-called global ambassador, a really nice way of describing a fund-raiser, but he also said that my active participation would serve to encourage patients: You've got a really positive story to tell, he said. This'll give you a platform to tell it.

Mitt told me the story of the world-renowned Dana-Farber Cancer Institute. Dr. Farber had made a lot of progress in fighting that disease, but at one point he realized he needed to find someone who could connect to the philanthropic community and get the attention of political leaders, so he enlisted Mary Lasker. With her husband, she founded the Lasker Foundation, and brought tremendous resources to the fight against cancer. At one time people were very reluctant to talk about cancer. The "Big C" they used to call it, and they'd whisper about people who had it. Mary Lasker relentlessly campaigned throughout the world, using the techniques of advertising and promotion, to bring attention and, more important, money to the fight—including the Charles A. Dana Foundation, and hence the name Dana-Farber. Mitt believed that, like Mary Lasker, I had the ability to bring people together, speak to political leaders, and make the necessary connections among different institutions, the private sector, and the government.

If I had any doubt about what my function would be, Dennis Selkoe explained it to a reporter. "We weren't looking for Ann and Mitt to create an endowment," he said, which by the way was a great relief to my wonderful husband. "That was never the idea. The thought was that she could use her passion and her ability to reach out to people all over the world to make our case that brain diseases shouldn't be accepted. Cancer and cardiac disease are way ahead of us in terms of getting the attention that can be converted into fund-raising; the brain has been more of a black box. If people die of a heart problem or a kidney problem or cancer, a pathologist already has permission to conduct an autopsy—but if someone dies of a neurologic disease, a family member has to sign a separate permission to allow the pathologist to examine the brain, as if there is something taboo or unusual about it. Frankly the mystery surrounding the brain is one reason we haven't made more progress. And I think Ann can help us get attention."

All these thoughts were incredibly flattering, and the concept really began taking shape in my mind.

Which is how the Ann Romney Center for Neurologic Diseases—note that we kept the two doctors' original "Neurologic"!—at Brigham and Women's Hospital was born. Long before I got involved, the place was unique, as it brought together doctors and scientists working in different neurologic fields in a way that had not been done before. As Dr. Weiner said, "This is a place where we have interactions that don't normally happen. And we have them every hour, every day."

The broad concept of the center is to have a single place where neurologic patients can get diagnoses, advice, and treatment, and if there is no treatment, they can participate in the ongoing research, as I'm doing, to find one. They can sign up for the studies and, if possible, the experiments. As Dr. Weiner explained, "What makes this center different is our integrated approach. By convening a global consortium of researchers and scientists working together across each of the five disease states, we are creating a novel and collaborative approach for biomedical research, which will lead to new breakthroughs, therapies, and clinical trials for patients."

The initial goal we set was to raise 50 million dollars, slightly more than the entire annual budget for the existing institute, which would be spent both on brick and mortar—the center is moving into a brand-new building—more technology, and the hiring of as many as fifty additional researchers. Mitt and I donated some seed money to help the center begin to grow.

Of course I recognize that my name is associated with politics, but this effort rises way above that, so we set out right at the beginning to make certain the center would be absolutely nonpolitical. One of the first people to join our absolutely nonpartisan board, for example, was Marc Mezvinsky, who is married to Chelsea Clinton and has a close relative with MS. In 2013 that relative went to see Dr. Weiner, who encouraged this person to become much more aggressive in their treatment. Also serving on the board is Robert Kennedy's grandson, Congressman Joseph P. Kennedy III; TV personality Meredith Vieira, whose husband, journalist Richard Cohen, was diagnosed with MS more than four decades ago; Mitt; Spencer Zwick; Montel Williams; and Fox Business Network host and expert Neil Cavuto, who has been diagnosed with the progressive form of the disease. "Having difficulty talking isn't good in my profession, but my wife welcomes it," Cavuto said, laughing. Although he usually memorizes his scripts in case he can't read the teleprompter while taping his show.

Near the conclusion of the dinner that we held to celebrate the announcement of the center, we asked several people to stand up spontaneously and talk about one of the five diseases and how it had impacted their lives. One of them was Nancy Frates, whose son Pete's battle with ALS was the inspiration for the Ice Bucket Challenge. This was the best possible example of "putting a face" on each disease. The emotional impact was truly astonishing: most of us in the room were crying, as much with empathy for the things that each of these people had suffered as with a kind of relief that someone was finally bringing together some of the best people in the world to mount a large and continuing attack on these enemies.

I'm the front woman. My primary job is to raise awareness of the existence of the center, and the challenges we all face from this array of neurologic enemies, and to emphasize the need for funding. A question that I have been asked by people who have connected my public visibility, my faith, and the center is whether I believe my getting MS was all part of a greater plan to put me in a position to help change countless lives. It is a fair question and it is easy to answer:

No.

I believe life is almost indiscriminate. Life happens. It hits us the way it hits us, and then we can choose to do with that reality whatever we choose. I don't see it as being part of any Grand Design. I don't think that God had a hand in this, that He reached down and decided, I'm going to make Ann sick and someday she's going to have a larger impact. But what I do believe is that we each have to play the hand we're dealt, and that life is a lot nicer for all of us if we help each other tote that heavy bag of rocks. The hope is that each of us can find a small niche in which we can make a difference. My brother Jim was able to see the lovely young life he was able to help save. And the center turned out to be the place where I could do the most to help. Fortunately I went into remission, and because of that I am able to bring people together as a force for good. I have always believed that each person doing a little will add up to a lot of change.

Mitt admits he is sometimes astonished to see the shy young girl he fell in love with in high school standing up in front of a large crowd addressing them forcefully. Here's a little secret: me, too. Several years ago while straightening our house, I found a photograph of me that was taken the first Christmas after I was diagnosed with MS. I'm sitting in a chair. The chair is gray, I'm wearing a gray sweater, my face is gray. My shoulders are hunched, and I seemed to be thoroughly defeated. When I looked at that picture, it brought me right back to how I felt at that time: gray. I was sad and deeply depressed. My future was bleak. I remembered those horrible feelings. Around me, everyone was getting ready for Christmas, and all I was capable of doing was sitting in that chair. After a few seconds I ripped up that picture. I ripped it into as many pieces as I could, telling myself, *I don't ever want to go back there again. I don't want to be in that dark place again, ever.* I wish now that I hadn't ripped up that photograph. I wish I could show it to anyone struggling with their burden—as I stand tall and tell them they have a future.

I'm the ultimate late bloomer. I got pushed into places I didn't want to go, but because of that, I grew. It was when I got put in a very uncomfortable situation that I realized, maybe for the first time, how much strength I had. Certainly because of the roads Mitt and I have followed, I had a public voice. I realized that I had the potential to influence the direction of the research and impact the lives of many people. For many years I had to lean on others, and now I had arrived at a place where they could lean on me.

I'm strong now, maybe stronger than I have ever been in my life, and I know I can help improve the quality of people's lives and support their fight against these terrible neurologic diseases. I'm thrilled to be able to get up and speak in front of an audience. I'm warning you, when there are people out there ready to donate money, don't get between me and a microphone. Where once I was hesitant, now I am ready. I know who I am, my feet are planted solidly on the ground. Nobody intimidates me, nobody.

Personally, I may be in remission, but like all of us, I'm never more than the next phone call away from being reminded how terrible these diseases are. There's an expression used in the fund-raising community: put a face on a disease. This means remind people that we are all affected in some way. Believe me, as far as neurologic diseases go, that's a reminder we don't need: none of us is ever very far away from these diseases, whether they affect us or the people we love. We got another call reminding us of just that in the summer of 2014, from Mitt's former chief of staff and campaign manager, Beth Myers. Beth is an extraordinary person who has been an active participant in the fight against neurologic diseases for years. One Saturday afternoon during that summer, she was simply having a drink on Nantucket when suddenly she went partially numb on her left side. Initially she thought it was a stroke. Physicians at Nantucket Hospital were not sure, but they thought it was a neurologic issue.

Beth and I spoke almost immediately, and I told her how important it was to see the right doctors. While she was her usual calm and commanding self, we both wanted her to get the best possible medical care as quickly as possible. She was airlifted by helicopter off Nantucket and told they were taking her to Mass General, another world-class hospital. That's where her treatment began.

It took the doctors there some time to diagnose her illness. Diagnosing neurologic diseases can be very tricky. It remains a sometimes inexact science. One hears from doctors a lot of *we don't know, we can't tell, this could be*, and worse, *we can't predict*. While this was going on for Beth, Mitt and I were with our family at Lake Winnipesaukee in New Hampshire. Beth came up to join us and we waited for her results together, spending time talking. There are a great number of neurologic diseases and conditions beyond the five being studied at the center, and there is little doubt that advances in any one of those diseases can eventually have a profound effect on any of the others.

Beth's disease is clever. It hides in the brain. When Dr. Weiner originally looked at her MRI results, he thought they looked pretty good, but in actuality they weren't so great. Eventually her doctors came to believe she probably has something called cerebral amyloid angiopathy, which is essentially a build-up of the same type of plaque Dr. Selkoe has been working with for decades, but in this disease the deposits are found in the blood vessels of the central nervous system. The result is a proclivity to bleeding in the brain. The prognosis is variable: the disease process could take years, but it sometimes leads to additional strokes. Like so many of these diseases the not knowing, the unpredictability of it, makes it even harder to deal with than those diseases about which so much more is known. Meanwhile, Beth is following the best of all possible paths: continuing to be Beth. While she is aware that at some point this chronic disease may be a problem, she is determined not to be defined or limited by it, and to continue to lead a happy, healthy, and productive life.

The research being done at the center may well prove important to Beth—and millions of other people who eventually will get involved in these battles. The more we learn about the brain, about those deposits, the more likely it is we will find the way to deal with them.

Having already explored some of this territory with both Natalie and me, Beth is very knowledgeable about it. But at these times it's always important to have your own Margo and Laraine, people you can talk to honestly and openly, who can help you deal with it. The first thing I told Beth was that eventually she was going to go to that dark place in her mind—and when she was there, as difficult as it was to believe and accept it, she had to focus on the fact that she was going to come back from there. Then I reminded her that as great as her doctors are, nobody, absolutely nobody, was going to pay as much attention to her getting well as she was. Take risks, I told her; get out of that comfort zone and try anything and everything. I gave her much of the same advice I had learned and lived by and passed along, but eventually it came down to one simple rule: Live your life. Don't let a diagnosis stop you from being you. Don't let your disease define you. While everyone has responsibilities they have to take care of, start sorting out those things you need or want to do from those things you don't want to do. Beth got it, and told me she had finally reached the point where if she didn't really want to do something, she didn't do it.

While Beth is being treated by the experts in her disease at Mass General, and is participating in studies, she also is paying close attention to the research being done at the center. The creation of the Ann Romney Center for Neurologic Diseases was announced in October 2014, although the formal dedication was delayed until the move into the brand-new building in 2016.

One of the first initiatives we've taken is the launching of a social media campaign entitled 50 Million Faces, a website (https://www.50millionfaces.org) and Twitter account (@50MillionFaces) where people affected by the five brain diseases being studied can share their stories. This includes families and caregivers as well as patients. Like so many Americans, I watched with delight as the Ice Bucket Challenge in 2014 brought incredible attention to, as well as raising about one hundred million dollars for, the fight against ALS. Mitt and I and all our boys, and most of our twenty-three grandchildren participated. Obviously you can't do something like that again, but it was amazing to watch it catch fire. We took the message from that and tried to figure out how to reach the most people possible to create a similar response.

Montel Williams and Jack Osborne, both of whom have MS, joined me in founding the site. The message we're trying to communicate is that we've all been wounded and we're all wearing our battle scars, but together we can go out and fight. It is incredibly important that anyone suffering from one of these diseases knows they are not alone. I remember feeling so terribly alone. It's an awful feeling, and if we can prevent people from the worst impact of that, we will have accomplished something. The stories that people have posted on the site and on Twitter are honest and tough and hopeful and, too often, sad. They are the stories of people who have shown tremendous courage. Some of them will make you cry. The stories are different, but they have one thing in common: they are the stories of people who have felt the effects of neurologic diseases and have joined with us to help find treatments and cures. As we hoped, they are putting a face, 50 million faces, to these diseases.

They include people such as Denise Hodgkins, who wrote:

> *I am writing this for my mother. The strong mother who worked and took care of three kids by herself . . . Loved us so much that every memory still makes me smile. This lovely person has progressive MS . . . She has been blind, she has been embarrassed for the falls in public, she has had to crawl to the restroom when her legs gave up on her . . . I have cringed when she would call and say she blacked*

out while shopping or was yelled at for parking in the handicap [spot] . . . I recently crawled into bed and curled into a ball after a very upsetting phone call when she told me how upset she was with the neurologist for he had the nerve to tell her to prepare for the worst.

"Just two years ago my husband was a research scientist, distinguished lecturer and competitive Ironman triathlete," writes Lina Clark. "Today he is fighting for his life. ALS has gained awareness but there is still no treatment! Clinical trials and drug development takes 10–15 years and costs tens of millions. This has to change . . ."

Patrick O'Keefe, thirty-three years old, wrote that he "has been able to fend off a primary brain tumor since being diagnosed in 2006. I have undergone three successful brain tumor resection surgeries and a few rounds of oral chemotherapy . . . I am one of the lucky ones who has had great care and a treatable form of this disease. I am married and the father of a beautiful 8 month old daughter . . . My biggest challenge is to compartmentalize my anxieties so it doesn't effect [*sic*] my job, my family, and my friendships. We need to get beyond just 'treatments' and find a 'cure' once and for all, so that so many don't have to face these challenges."

While the immediate focus of the center is on the five diseases, 50 Million Faces is rapidly becoming the community center for people with any one of the too many different neurologic diseases. Amy Jeanette Benitez was diagnosed with myasthenia gravis in 2012, when she was twenty-one years old, and was transformed "from the girl with the smile from ear to ear to looking frozen. Daily gym days are gone forever! Struggling to comb my own hair, dressing myself, picking up my own legs to step or passing on dinner with a loved one 'cause you know you can't chew or swallow your food properly . . . I have MG. MG doesn't have me!"

These contributions often are written by friends and caregivers, who pay tribute to people like "My friend Aaron Loder [who] fought ALS for 11 years. He lost the battle on Monday [April 2015] but we will never give up the fight." And they come from everywhere in the world, including really close to home. Dr. Weiner posted a photograph of himself with his mother, and wrote, "Here's my mother and I in the Colorado Rockies before she developed Alzheimer's disease. She knew I was a 'famous doctor' working on multiple sclerosis. After she developed Alzheimer's disease her mind became clouded and all she knew was that she had a brain disease and that her son was a brain doctor. She said to me, 'Howie, can't you help me with this?' Unfortunately, there was nothing I could do at that time. But now we can do something through the work we are doing here at the Ann Romney Center so others won't have to experience what she went through."

Our goal was probably best expressed by Ginger Maner, who wrote, "I have been fighting the Monster since 2008 when I lost my right eyesight. Since then MS has impacted my life in ways that I never clearly thought it would . . . My biggest fear is that my daughters will end up with MS. I do not want them or anyone else to ever hear the words, 'You have MS' again. MS doesn't just impact you, but everyone in your life. I am very thankful that steps are being made to bring more awareness and help, not only to MS, but the other diseases."

I'm inspired by Ginger "fighting the Monster." The only way a war is won against a formidable foe is with a large and committed army. Those of us who have been touched by neurologic diseases are the infantry of that army (especially those like me who have been given a temporary reprieve from its most debilitating symptoms). Doctors and researchers are the intelligence officers, analyzing where to aim the weapons. Pharmaceutical and imaging companies build those weapons and supply the ammo. In the past, it felt like our army was failing not only to make progress, but even to coordinate and collaborate on a battle plan. Today, the wounded like Ginger Maner are standing up and fighting, the researchers are sharing their insights, and the corporations are aiming in the right direction for progress. GE's Jeffrey Immelt announced that his company is moving out of financial services and redirecting its investment toward industrial businesses like health care, where half a billion dollars will be devoted to neurological research. Treatments have already changed the battlefield, and new, more promising weapons are in the pipeline.

Being part of an army changes a person, particularly when you came to that army involuntarily. My family has noticed a change in me as I have fought my disease. I am more determined, more assertive, more inquisitive, less willing to accept excuses and delays, more dependent on God, and far more appreciative for every good thing in life and love. In this, I know I'm not alone: many people I have come to know that have endured hardship reflect that in some ways they are grateful for their trial. It brought them greater understanding and revealed personal qualities they would not have developed any other way. No, we don't celebrate the hardship and pain, but we do recognize what it has brought out in us.

Even so, there is pain and suffering that never heals: those who have lost a child or spouse, another family member, or a friend always endure a hollow in their heart. Nor can any one person expect to escape permanently from sorrow and hardship. As people first experience a burden, they often wonder "why me?" The answer is straightforward: "Because you are a mortal living in a mortal world, because everyone suffers loss and pain and ultimately death." What distinguishes us is how we respond to the trials we confront. I cannot judge those who succumb to depression and despair, who slip into the shadow of defeat. I was there myself for a time. I have been in a very dark hole, if just for a moment, but long enough to have been taught by a cruel teacher.

But I also know that some burdens, even ones that appear overwhelmingly heavy, are sometimes borne with courage and vitality. Nelson Mandela endured years upon years of prison and emerged as a loving and forgiving man who was able to transform a nation and inspire the world. Stephanie Nielson had 80 percent of her body burned, suffered excruciating pain, watched her children shrink in horror from the sight of her, and then rebuilt her life as a mother, wife, and author.

I have noted earlier that at a very dark time in my battle

with MS, I was given a blessing by Elder Henry Eyring and by my husband. Among the words they spoke were these: "The Lord has accepted your sacrifice, Ann. You will go through a healing process, and through that process you will gain greater appreciation and understanding of the atonement of Jesus Christ." The healing has indeed been a process, and that process will continue. My understanding of Christ's atonement has also grown, as promised. I know that many people do not believe that Jesus was the Son of God or even that he was a divine personage. But for them, too, there are lessons from His atonement.

Jesus was God—or, if you are a nonbeliever, a man who was the personification of all that is good and noble. He cared for the poor and the sick. He extolled the outcast Samaritan and criticized the haughty Pharisees. He gave sermons of love and forgiveness that inspire to this day. In the history of humankind, there could not be a being less deserving of crucifixion. But He willingly subjected Himself to death, entering the city He knew would kill him. He confronted his peril. We, too, can confront our disease and despair.

I am a soldier in this army, continuing to learn about these diseases and about the people who fight them on every single level. While I'm not going to be the person looking into a microscope who one day finds that key that changes so many lives forever, I am going to be working as hard as I can to make certain that day happens, and soon. The one promise I can make is simple, and I believe it with all my heart: hope is on the way.

Afterword: The Work of the Ann Romney Center

IN EARLY 2013, it seemed impossible to believe that a decade had raced by from the day Mitt was inaugurated as the governor of Massachusetts to the conclusion of our final campaign. We had crammed a lifetime in political years into such a brief span of time. It also remained amazing and exciting to me how far I had come physically since those darkest days. My disease was essentially in remission. I had remained in contact with Dr. Weiner, visiting the center at least once each year for a checkup and, like every MS patient, following the progress of researchers in Boston and around the world as they hunted down and tried to destroy my monster. The fear that I'm always one day away from another attack has never dissipated. It's still there in the corner of my mind. I know I can be right back at that dark place instantly, and honestly, I don't know if I have the energy to fight it like I did before. So when I visit

Dr. Weiner in Boston, while I always enjoy seeing him, it isn't a social call. I want to know what's in the pipeline for people like me, who have already been diagnosed and are fighting this thing, as well as those people who someday will turn a corner and be confronted by this disease.

The organizational structure of Dr. Weiner and Dr. Selkoe's lab was always a little confusing for me. They each ran their own centers; Dr. Weiner saw MS patients at the MS Clinical Research Unit at Brigham and Women's Hospital, while Dr. Selkoe saw Alzheimer's patients in his unit. In addition, they served as codirectors of the Center for Neurologic Diseases, where cutting-edge research and experimentation were being conducted.

It seemed that each time I visited through the years, I could see the MS research unit growing. What was necessary for the next step, Dr. Weiner knew, was a facility dedicated to the clinical study of MS. And Dr. Selkoe always pointed out, one day for Alzheimer's, too. Dr. Weiner needed a building in which the examining rooms, infusion rooms, physical therapy rooms, office space, storage space, and all the research labs would be a short walk away— and, he always added somewhat wistfully, an MRI for the exclusive use of MS patients.

Weiner raised four million dollars to fund the MS center, but he had been unable to find the right space. When substantial room became available above the Harvard Medical School bookstore, directly across the street from the hodgepodge of space the center then occupied, Dr. Weiner knew it was perfect. But there was considerable competition for that space, and every competitor believed his or her need was greatest. I've known Howard Weiner for almost two decades, and in that time I've never seen him lose his temper once. His intensity and his sense of purpose, and sense of humor, had always successfully masked whatever anger or frustration he was feeling. But from the stories I've heard, this was not the case in this situation: Apparently he let loose his temper. He threw a major-league tantrum, yelling and screaming for almost an hour, explaining why he both needed and deserved that space for a new MS center. Days later, he even sent a dying member of the hospital board, a supporter of the center, to see the administrator to plead his case. It worked. The new MS center, complete with that all-important MRI that I would get to know, opened on April 25, 2000. At the dedication, Dr. Weiner told the staff, at that time slightly more than one hundred twenty-five people, "This is where we'll stay until we find a cure for MS."

The Neurologic Center, the place where the experimentation is taking place, also has continued to grow. Presently it consists of twenty-two different labs and about two hundred fifty people working at the bench conducting experiments. A modern lab doesn't look anything at all like a war room, but that's actually what this is. From here, science wages war with disease. There's nothing very exciting to look at. It's mostly long tables with all the equipment normally associated with scientific research sitting on top or on shelves. There are books and microscopes, large pieces of equipment, copy machines, and computers, lots of computers. Generally it's quiet, but every time I visited, there seemed to be the hum of optimism in the air. And every

time I saw Dr. Weiner he seemed about to burst with excitement over the results of some test or study. "For the first
time, in this decade we really have seen patients doing better," he told me once. "I now have patients coming in whom
I can examine, give them an MRI and other tests, and be
able to tell with certainty whether or not they had this
disease. More than that, I was able to separate my patients
into two groups, easy patients and hard patients. In the
past, they were all hard patients."

If I had to get this disease, at least my timing turned out
to be fortuitous. The year I was diagnosed, the theme of the
annual American Academy of Neurology, then meeting in
Boston, was "Revolution in Neurology"—and it did mark
the beginning of a revolution in research and treatment. A
few years before I was diagnosed, the first real drugs for
treating the disease had recently become available, although
they were still in the very early stages and no one seemed too
excited about them. As Dr. Weiner told me, if I hadn't
responded to steroids, we would have tried those drugs. But
by 2000 about one hundred clinical trials for new medicines
were planned, in progress, or recently completed.

Incredible progress had been made since the time I was
diagnosed. Without question more advances were made in
diagnosing and treating MS in the last decade or so than
in the previous history combined—although, in some cases
at least, the disease still remains very difficult to diagnose.
I have heard of diagnosed cases in which after several years
the diagnosis of MS turned out to be in error, and in fact
it was some other neurologic disease. When I was diagnosed, so little was really known about the disease that the

old expression "Diagnose and adios" covered the "range" of available treatments. Treatment often meant doing the best to manage symptoms such as urinary complications and joint pain. That has changed completely. Investigators have picked up the scent and been relentless in pursuing the clues, successfully changing the treatment landscape, and even making the hope of a vaccine or a cure realistic.

I've asked Howard Weiner what my expectations should be. Will I pick up my phone one day and hear him tell me, "We got it! We got it figured out!" Probably not, he cautioned me. Most likely there will be a long series of small incremental steps, in figuring out not just MS and Alzheimer's, but all neurologic diseases. Among those things that I personally believe we're going to see, and maybe even soon, is nerve restoration, the stimulation of existing limbs, and amazing advances in the use of artificial limbs. I think we'll also be able to reduce the number and severity of incidents, but as for curing any of these diseases, from everything I've learned, that's still a long way in the future.

While the most important and tantalizing question—what causes MS?—has not yet been answered, much has been learned about it. It's generally accepted by researchers that MS is an autoimmune disease in which for some unknown reason the body's own immune system warriors, the white blood cells, attack the brain and spinal cord, specifically the myelin sheath protecting the neurons. One of the best theories about why this happens is that the immune system initially responds to a virus that in some important ways resembles the cells in the myelin sheath, and then mistakenly continues to attack healthy cells. Mitt and I have often wondered, for example, if the very bad flu I had several weeks before the onset of my disease had anything to do with it. Is it possible that it caused my immune system to go out of whack and turn on my body? We'll never know the answer to that question.

Unlike with some viruses, though, there is no evidence that MS can be transmitted from one person to another. Recently, scientists have begun focusing on the gut as playing some type of important role in causing a range of immune diseases. The gut is the body's largest immune system, command and control for the immune system. An estimated seven hundred trillion bacteria call it home—although no one has made a definitive count. There is some speculation that diet may even play a role. In Japan, for instance, where MS once was relatively rare, the number of new cases has coincided with significant changes in the diets of the Japanese people. Also, there seems to be some evidence that vitamin D may play a role, as the number of diagnosed cases seems to rise as the amount of available sunlight, the source of vitamin D, decreases. The farther people live from the equator, the more likely they are to be afflicted with the disease. No one yet knows why someone like me suddenly and without warning, and seemingly without any triggering event, would have been diagnosed with MS.

At least some of the most perplexing questions have been answered. Among the most puzzling mysteries that has been solved is why some people responded to some therapies while others did not. Why did I have such a dramatic response to treatment and was able to continue leading a happy and relatively healthy life while other people who got the same or similar treatment ended up in a wheelchair? Dr. Weiner published a paper in the 1980s reporting that he had successfully used chemotherapy to stop the progression of the disease. It created a stir in the medical community, because until then there had been very little progress made in fighting MS. But a decade later, when Canadian researchers tried to repeat his results and failed miserably, his discovery suddenly became quite controversial and his reputation was damaged. For Dr. Weiner, it was especially frustrating. He knew he'd found something that had dramatically helped some patients but apparently didn't have the same impact on others. "I knew we were right," he said. "But I couldn't figure out why. We couldn't find the right key to turn." That's probably why the doctor I saw initially followed the conservative and widely accepted protocol: go home and only after your disease progresses can we do anything to help.

One of the very basic tenets of research, going all the way back to the beginning of science, is that an experimental result is not considered valid until it has been repeated by someone else following the same recipe. The history of science is replete with people who gained attention by claiming to have made some amazing discovery, only to be exposed as frauds when those results couldn't be repeated by researchers working independently.

Dr. Weiner eventually concluded that chemo worked mostly when it was given very early in the progression of the disease. In response to questions about his results, he had a list of patients, eventually including me, who were early in their disease whose lives had changed and maybe been saved by aggressive treatment. But the question remained: Why? What allowed some people to lead almost normal lives while others ended up crippled and in wheelchairs?

What became more and more apparent during this research was that, in fact, there were two different forms of the disease, relapsing and remitting, and progressive. Relapsing MS means that people have attacks and recover. Progressive MS, as it sounds, continues to get worse, symptoms accumulate over long periods of time without ever getting better, and there are few effective treatments. Before the therapies now used to fight relapsing MS, about three quarters of patients would eventually develop a progressive form of the disease. Most of the research being done, and all the successful research, has been centered on relapsing MS. Suddenly Dr. Weiner had at least a partial answer to the question of why certain patients responded to his treatments while others did not. There were two markedly different forms of MS. It had become clear that chemo and steroids were effective only in the relapsing stages of the disease and probably not at all effective in fighting the progressive form once it had taken root. (Clearly the Canadian researchers who refuted Dr. Weiner's results had been treating patients with the progressive form of the disease.) Where I was so fortunate is that Dr. Weiner was able to treat me in the early stages of my disease, when steroids still would have had an effect. But as I have said, like all MS patients, I live with the knowledge that my reprieve is only temporary, that at some unknown time, for some unknown cause, it may strike again and this time harder.

The discovery of the two forms of MS led to one of the main unresolved questions about the disease: what causes the manageable relapsing disease to be transformed into the far more aggressive and debilitating progressive disease? For some reason, in some patients, the disease suddenly shifts gear into high-performance mode and races forward.

The problem with most animal models being used when Dr. Weiner did his initial study was that they would have an attack and then recover, which was the pattern of the relapsing form of the disease. But while people with progressive MS do recover from attacks, their symptoms continue to get worse, and for many years there was no animal model that mimicked this. Eventually, though, by adapting laboratory mice bred for diabetes studies, scientists in Dr. Weiner's MS unit were finally able to develop an animal model that successfully followed the pattern of the progressive form of the disease, which has allowed some cutting-edge research to be done. For the first time a real experimental platform existed.

Another essential advance at the beginning of the new century was made in magnetic resonance imaging. For the first time, MRIs permitted researchers to look inside the brain and see exactly what it was they were fighting—and more important, how it responded to specific treatments. It meant that they no longer were flying blind. When they tested a new drug, for example, they actually could "see" the response. In fact, the FDA has not approved a single drug to fight MS that did not ultimately show a positive effect in an MRI. Maybe equally significant, MRIs have allowed researchers to track the progression of the disease. When I go in for my annual checkup, for example, I always have an MRI to make certain there have been no substantive changes in my disease.

The advances in imaging, in being able to see the enemy, represent a significant step forward. Dr. Weiner's partner at the center, Dennis Selkoe, spent his career studying Alzheimer's disease and has dissected numerous brains. He's spent years peering into microscopes and became respected as the leading Alzheimer's researcher in the world. But it wasn't until 2002, until these new imaging techniques became available, that he was able finally to "look" into a living brain and watch what was happening over time.

This ability to watch the progression of a disease in the human brain and spinal cord was a key factor in the establishment of the MS unit's CLIMB study, which stands for Comprehensive Longitudinal Investigations of Multiple Sclerosis. Begun in 2000 at Brigham and Women's Hospital, this observational, fact-gathering study looks at more than two thousand MS patients, including me, whom it has been following for a ten- to twenty-year period. It is the most comprehensive study of this kind ever done on MS.

Unlike other diseases, such as cancer, MS does not have a community that treats patients according to common protocols of therapy. That's why even today different doctors treat patients differently. One purpose of the CLIMB study is to find those common factors in the development, treatment, and outcome for the entire universe of MS patients.

Each participant in the study is following his or her own physician's directives. Every six months, sometimes once a year, the center collects information about their neurologic status, their MRI status, and several biological samples, including blood and genetics samples. It also tracks the progress of the disease from its onset, including relapse rates, treatments, disability scores, and quality-of-life issues.

This was the first time a large MS database had been compiled, and the MRI exams serve as a visual baseline. Similar studies have proven tremendously beneficial in the past, as previously unknown patterns and connections can be derived from the information gathered. The famed Framingham Heart Study, which began in 1948, collected data every two years from more than five thousand men and women from the town of Framingham, Massachusetts. The goal was to use those data to try to understand which factors contributed to heart disease. The researchers wanted to track the habits of those people who later developed cardiovascular problems and those who remained heart healthy. That study continues today, with more people recruited over various periods since then, and has been one of the major contributors to our understanding of heart disease. It was the Framingham study that successfully identified high blood pressure, high blood cholesterol, smoking, obesity, diabetes, and physical inactivity as major risk factors.

Howard Weiner compares his study to the polio experiment of 1954 in which four hundred thousand kids were vaccinated and a large number of kids received a placebo. Nine months later researchers saw who got polio and who didn't, and the experiment was stopped and every child then got the vaccination. But this wasn't going to be nine months. As he says of MS, "This disease progresses very slowly, so it isn't how a patient is in two years; it's what happens over ten years or even twenty years."

The CLIMB study has the same ambitious goals as the Framingham study or the polio experiment—figure out what treatment has worked and what has failed and try to understand the factors that contributed to that result. I'm absolutely thrilled to be part of it. Like every patient diagnosed with a complex disease, I want to do something, anything, to help other people diagnosed with it. The frustration has been that there was so little I could do. Participating in the CLIMB study has at least made me feel that something worthwhile might come out of my illness. It really was the beginning of my involvement in helping to fight this thing.

The study has already proven its worth. When a new medicine is introduced, for example, it has enabled researchers to track its value in real time. In certain cases that also has allowed scientists to understand how to use those medicines without causing side effects. And based on papers that the CLIMB study has published, some doctors have changed their methods of treatment.

The results of the CLIMB study have already been impressive. Researching this disease sometimes seems like an archeological dig—the farther down you go, the more mysteries you uncover. A subset of progressive MS has been called malignant MS, which means it progresses unusually quickly. Within five years from the onset, for example, patients may be walking with a cane and their symptoms continue to get worse. About 12 percent of the participants in the study fit into that category. Among the proven risk factors for malignant MS is smoking. It became pretty clear that this patient population benefitted from early and aggressive treatment.

One of the initial conclusions, which was already pretty well known, was that as hard as MS is to diagnose accurately and treat, physicians were using a number of different clinical and MRI biomarkers to monitor the effect of various treatments. The numbers showed that patients who had a higher number of brain lesions when initially diagnosed, logically were more likely to fail to respond to treatment and had to be watched more closely and treated more aggressively.

What came somewhat as a surprise is that MS is often present in the body for many years before it can no longer be ignored. About 3 percent of adult MS patients experienced their first symptoms of MS during their childhood or adolescence, but were not diagnosed with the disease. The increased awareness among physicians that isolated symptoms could be signs of a serious disease conceivably would lead to an earlier diagnosis, which would mean beginning treatment sooner—which obviously could have major benefits for the rest of a patient's life. CLIMB study statistics also indicate that those children who are diagnosed with MS generally experience two to three times as many relapses as adults. By the end of 2014, more than fifty papers had been published based on data collected in the CLIMB study. Equally important, Google is in discussion with the MS Center to use its medical computational abilities to drill down into the statistics to try to find additional correlations.

One of the major initiatives currently being pursued as part of the CLIMB study is to develop so-called biomarkers, which are used to monitor the progress of the disease and are crucial for conducting studies. An MRI is the most widely used biomarker; it replaced an analysis of spinal fluid, which was obtained through sometimes painful spinal taps. There is considerable emphasis on developing a blood test for MS that will allow physicians to determine quickly, painlessly, and inexpensively whether the disease is active in a patient, whether it is the relapsing or progressive form, and if and how the patient is responding to various medications. Throughout the history of the CLIMB study, the center has collected and has available more than seventy-five thousand blood samples from more than three thousand patients at all stages of the disease. A recent breakthrough was the discovery of micro-RNA circulating in the bloodstream that can be used to diagnose the disease and determine its stage.

Like so many other chronic diseases, in addition to taking a physical toll, MS also can cause serious psychological damage. In fact, this disease affects every aspect of your life—and often, because many MS patients look perfectly healthy and may be able to lead close-to-normal lives, other people just don't get it. Believe me, I've seen people question MS patients who dared park in a handicapped spot; I've heard people say about me, "Well, she doesn't look sick." I know that some people actually believe my disease had some political benefit. I understand people think the exhaustion can be resolved simply by our getting more sleep. Many MS patients have experienced that same reaction: "You don't look sick. Why can't you just . . . just do anything." If people could only see what was going on inside.

On those nights I was just too tired to go to a scheduled event or those days when I had to stop campaigning, I really felt I was letting people down. When that happens it is incredibly frustrating. Fortunately, another aspect of the CLIMB study is attempting to assess the social damage inflicted by MS. Obviously the disease can make it difficult for people to keep and hold a job. The rate of unemployment for MS patients has been as high as 80 percent. That's a huge number. Those people who are working also may experience greatly increased absenteeism as well as what is called presenteeism, meaning reduced productivity while at work. About half the working people in the study reported that their productivity had been affected, which also meant that the possibility of advancing in their field or getting that raise was limited. As researchers reported, MS patients felt constrained in the amount or kind of work they did, they accomplished a lot less than they intended, and they were not as careful. And depression, greater fatigue, anxiety, and decreased quality of life could all be associated with that reduced productivity.

My annual visits to the MS Center, as well as my occasional phone calls for advice about certain issues, kept me connected to Dr. Weiner. And as I got to know him I realized what a truly unique person he is. There have been times, for example, when he might have made requests to me that would have benefitted the center. But he has never done so, not once. During Mitt's term as governor, for example, he never asked me for a single thing. Politics never entered our discussions because, as he pointed out, "MS is an ecumenical disease: it doesn't discriminate between people with different political beliefs."

Year by year, advances continue to be made. In 2003, for example, researchers in Italy began transplanting cells to facilitate nerve tissue repair in mice with MS. A 2004 study conducted by the MS Society indicated that African Americans tend to get the more aggressive form of the disease. Scientists from around the world came together in 2007 at a Stem Cell Research Summit to map a strategy for attacking the disease with stem cells; and that same year, many genes were linked to susceptibility to MS. An international force meeting in 2009 published guidelines to enable physicians to differentiate MS from look-alike disease. A major study to assess the value of vitamin D supplements began in 2011. By 2014 the first clinical trials of myelin repair strategies progressed into phase two. And seemingly every year, new drugs have been approved by the FDA to fight this disease.

While there still are no therapies that will repair or restore the damage, at least doctors can now map out a battle plan to slow down the disease's progression. There is currently an array of medicines used to respond to the initial onset and to change the course of the disease, to deal with relapses and to manage the variety of symptoms. Attacks or relapses are caused by inflammation in the central nervous system, and the best treatment for that, it turns out, is steroids. While there is little evidence that steroids have long-term benefits, they do beat back an attack pretty rapidly.

The first drug therapy to fight MS, interferon, became available only in 1993, although few physicians prescribed it. But by 2015, the FDA had approved twelve different drugs for recurring MS that helped blunt the severity of the attacks and the disease's progression. All these drugs, unfortunately, target the relapsing form of the disease. Each works by affecting a different area of the immune system. Because MS treatments have to be tailored to the individual patient, the more effective drugs there are, the better the chance that early intervention will prevent the disease from progressing.

There also are other drugs to deal with all the symptoms, although these are not aimed solely or directly at MS patients. Thirteen different drugs on the market can be used to fight bladder problems, for example. There are drugs that help patients combat spasticity and walking problems, drugs for sexual problems and depression, drugs for bowel problems and tremors. Many of these, of course, are common and popular drugs that are widely used no matter the underlying disease, such as Zoloft to fight depression. But all of them have given MS doctors weapons they never had before.

I know how fortunate I have been. As Dr. Weiner told me, "In your lifetime as an MS patient, we've seen MS changing from an untreatable disease without a lot of medicine options to a disease where every couple of years a new medicine became available—although still only for the remitting form. The main problem is understanding the side effects of these different medicines. We don't know yet who should get what medicine or how to give them without causing the side effects, and figuring that out is one of the specific goals of the CLIMB study."

One of the exciting developments to come out of Dr. Weiner's lab is a nasal vaccine that in very early testing has been shown to be effective against progressive forms of MS. Most current treatments work by turning the immune system on to attack and destroying the enemy, T-cells. Dr. Weiner and his associate Dr. Lior Mayo, who joined the lab in 2010, wondered about a different approach to fight progressive MS by inducing and then enhancing the immune system's ability to regulate itself. They created a nasal vaccine using an antibody called anti-CD3, which was originally developed to fight organ rejection after a kidney transplant. It works by secreting an anti-inflammatory substance. Dr. Mayo found that these nasal drops actually halted the progression of the disease in animal models, successfully reducing the scope of an attack and the damage to the myelin sheath and the nerves. If it continues to prove successful, it would be one of the first treatments for progressive MS.

Another important discovery made in the lab was a potential vaccine for Alzheimer's disease. Dr. Dennis Selkoe was conducting an experiment in which he injected animals with the amyloid-beta peptide (A-beta), a substance found in the plaque that accumulates in the brains of Alzheimer's patients. He wasn't the first scientist to do this. This type of experimentation had been going on since at least 1999. When animal models were given a combination of the peptide and an adjuvant (a substance that turns on the immune system, causing it to respond), they got an unexpected result: While some of the "patients" died, others developed a condition that mimicked MS. There was no logical reason for this, and both Weiner and Selkoe became intrigued. For more than five years they tried to figure out the mechanism. Eventually they injected their Alzheimer's mouse models with this facsimile MS, and something totally unexpected happened: It cleared all the A-beta from the brain. It actually made Alzheimer's plaque disappear, and disappear completely, leaving the animals with this form of MS. Selkoe's theory was that the appearance of MS triggered the system to make antibodies against A-beta in the brain. The animal's immune system had successfully been activated to attack and destroy the Alzheimer's-causing plaque.

Howard Weiner and Dennis Selkoe were close friends and medical associates for decades, but each had found his own specialty and rose to the top of his field. While from time to time there had been some overlap in their work, this was the first time their two passions came together so perfectly. "Dennis asked me to come into the lab to look at something," Dr. Weiner remembers. "'Look at this,' he said. 'But I'm not going to tell you which is which.' When I followed his instructions, I almost couldn't believe what I was looking at. The A-beta was being cleared. 'Howard, oh my God,' he said excitedly and gave me a big hug."

A similar experiment being conducted in another lab, which was published first, showed the same results. The big difference between the two experiments was that the other lab was injecting the A-beta antibody, while at Brigham it was being given as a nasal spray. The group that developed the injectable form of the adjuvant received permission from the FDA to conduct live trials. When they did, unfortunately, some of the participants died, while others got the MS-like disease. The FDA immediately shut down the experiment, which prevented Selkoe and Weiner from testing their nasal vaccine on humans.

Still, a failed experiment can provide a lot of vital information. Ethically you can't treat Alzheimer's by giving people MS, so Weiner and Selkoe began wondering if they could isolate the factor independent from the MS that was clearing the plaque and use that to treat the disease. After almost four years of work, they developed an adjuvant that appeared to stimulate the immune system without causing MS. Rather than the adjuvant traditionally used in MS treatments, they substituted the adjuvant commonly used to develop influenza vaccines. This adjuvant had already been proven safe in humans. And it worked. It did not cause MS in animals and it cleared out the A-beta. By 2015 the nasal vaccine for Alzheimer's was in the early stages of testing.

One additional and especially important assessment to come out of the lab and the CLIMB study was a compilation of the different ways patients adjusted to their MS diagnosis. After decades of working with MS patients Dr. Weiner had been witness to the great variety of strategies people had adopted to deal with their new reality. While not all of them worked, a lot did. As I read this list of common and successful strategies, I realized that, without knowing it, I had pretty much done each of these things.

This is a pretty good checklist for dealing not just with MS, but as so many others have learned, with any bag of rocks:

Deal with your depression. The first thing almost everyone has to deal with is the natural depression that comes with any significant and negative change in your life. How well I remember those days after my diagnosis, the feeling that my life was over and it was only a question of how much I would suffer. Depression in those circumstances is normal, but when it lasts too long or drastically changes your behavior, it can be debilitating. There are different ways to deal with depression, including taking antidepressant medications, seeking counseling, exercising—and following the subsequent advice in this list.

Make and strengthen connections with others. When I was diagnosed, I had not only Mitt and our family, but also friends like Laraine. When I needed it most, I had Margo and the girls in the barn, who took me into their world and would not let me wallow in self-pity. I remember my original doctor suggested that I join an MS support group. I decided not to do that, instead unexpectedly finding so much of the social support I needed in the world of dressage.

Make achievable goals. Setting realizable goals will provide a feeling of accomplishment. Stephanie Nielson made her own simple list of the things she used to do before her plane accident, from changing a diaper to climbing a hill, and checked them off one by one as she accomplished each of them. My list was simple, too. I wanted to make dinner for my family, become a better rider, and eventually be good enough to compete on a high level in dressage. I also wanted to walk just a little farther every day than I had the day before. I set both short-term and long-term goals, what I wanted to get done in the next day or so and what I wanted to accomplish at some indeterminate time in the future. And while I didn't write them down, they were always there just ahead of me. And when I accomplished even one of the small ones, I always had a great feeling of achievement that reinforced my belief that my health was, at least partially, in my hands and that I was doing something to fight the monster.

Identify your strengths. Dr. Weiner noted that his patients were able to locate and identify their strengths; they often did so, he added, by remembering how they'd dealt with problems in the past. I was fortunate enough to have certain traits that proved important to me, including determination, a competitive spirit, and a strong work ethic. While each of these was incredibly important, my biggest strength might have been the role models I had in my parents and my in-laws. These were four remarkable people. In almost every trying situation, I could look into my memory and find some sort of guiding value. Both my father and George Romney had overcome tremendous obstacles to reach great success; both my mother and Lenore Romney were stylish, loving, supportive, and independent women. When I was down, I would remember my mother who, when she knew she was dying, refused our offer that she stay with us and allow us to take care of her, because she would never have allowed herself to become a burden to anyone else. Or I would remember my father, who refused to allow his failures in business to keep him from his eventual success. I would think about George Romney, who celebrated his love for his family by taking each of his grandchildren on a drive across America to visit historic sites after they turned twelve; and Lenore, who when asked why she accepted the challenge of running for the Senate against a popular incumbent said simply, "If not me, who?"

Take action. Dr. Weiner and his team became active in their fight against this disease. "It's not enough to talk," he said. "One must do something, particularly about MS." While he suggested that I do anything, from becoming involved in fund-raising to mentoring someone with MS, I followed the good advice I had been given and experimented with alternate and holistic therapies—to be used in addition to, not in place of, sound medical treatments. That's how I found my wonderful Fritz. In doing so, I let down barriers and was willing to try things I had so easily dismissed in the past. I also started riding again, which in my case made such a substantial difference. It was a challenge and a joy, and became the bridge to my new life.

Express gratitude. This is another way of pointing out how important it is to direct your focus as much as possible to the positive things in your life. I never forgot for an instant how fortunate I was to be married to a supportive man, to be surrounded by a loving family and supportive friends, and to have the resources to pay for my treatment. Even during my darkest moments, I was able to see a flicker of light, and eventually it grew bigger and brighter. I've had the opportunity to meet many other people carrying heavy weights, and I have always been amazed by their resiliency. When I meet people struggling with issues, the first thing they want to do is share photos of their children or grand-children with me. I know that it isn't always easy to do this. There are moments when that bag of rocks gets so heavy that people wonder if it's worth carrying it any farther. Yet those moments pass, and taking note of those things in your life that are positive will help you get through them.

Use your faith or spirituality. There are questions that can't be answered by science or personal experience, and "why" may be the most difficult one of all. At times it can be greatly beneficial to stop struggling to answer that question and find contentment in your version of faith and spiritu-ality. That sustenance may come from an organized religion or from nature or from your own set of beliefs. While my religion has always been my touchstone, the awe and the extraordinary peace that I experienced while sitting on a rooftop with my father looking into the night sky has re-mained an essential part of my character. Dr. Weiner writes that faith and spirituality help his patients remember that "there is much possibility of healing, even when there is no cure." What often can be derived from beliefs and ex-periences is optimism, a feeling that there is so much more around us than we know or understand. There were moments when I rode slowly through a mountain forest and simply looked around at the extraordinary beauty and knew for certain that miracles do happen.

Maintain hope. It is essential for your future well-being that you maintain hope. No matter what the circumstances, maintain hope. While campaigning, as often as possible I tried to meet with those people with MS who came to our rallies. I wanted them to see how well I was doing, to remind them that there is hope for our whole community. And the message I delivered was always some version of "Hang in there, help is on the way." And it is. In the 1920s Americans by the millions looked in the mirror every day and repeated the self-affirmation written by Emile Coué, "Every day, in every way, I'm getting better and better," and they continued to repeat it until they began to believe it and it made them feel better. Well, it is a fact that every day, in every way, we *are* getting closer and closer to cures and treatments for our most devastating diseases. We have more support, better experimental equipment, and dedicated researchers working every day to find answers. There is no question about it; help is on the way.

Give. Giving your time, your experience, and your strength allows you to engage with other people. While great satisfaction comes from the act of giving itself, equally important is how giving forces you to engage in the world. Too often people who face challenges don't want to participate in the world; they want to be left alone. Forcing yourself to give whatever it is you have to offer can change your entire attitude. It doesn't matter what it is. In many situations the most valuable thing you can give—for yourself even more than the recipient—is your time. One of the depressing realities for people facing serious issues is the recognition that the world continues to move forward without them. Forcing yourself to participate in that world, even when you don't feel great, can make a huge difference.

Use humor. Something funny happened on the way to the hospital. Okay, it probably didn't. But as Dr. Weiner points out, it is really important that we don't cut ourselves off from the full range of emotions, especially humor. Numerous studies have shown that humor can relieve stress, help stimulate your immune system, and even reduce pain. I will never forget sitting in my first doctor's office with Mitt as that physician responded to Mitt's question about intimacy by telling us about a couple who maintained a relationship by touching pinkies—and then the surge of humor I felt later when Mitt and I were standing together and he entwined my pinkie in his.

Experience the full range of emotions. Maybe the best remark about dealing with all of life's challenges came from my seventy-two-year-old mother as she was hunched over the wheel of her Pontiac GTO. She was caught in traffic and started screaming about bad drivers. "Ugh," she said in frustration, "these old people!" My brother Jim, sitting in the passenger seat, laughed and pointed out, "But Mom, aren't you old?" Being old was not something she could change, but, as she responded, "But I'm not slow!" The other emotions count too. It's not only okay to cry, it's important to cry. It's important to feel the entire range of emotions. I can't tell you how angry and frustrated I got at times, but letting it all out rather than pretending it wasn't there or holding it inside made a big difference for me. I can say it's a good thing I don't curse, because at times, when my horse wasn't responding to me and I let loose everything that had been pent up inside, I would not have been pleasant to be around. Cutting yourself off from emotions is the same as cutting yourself off from the world.

Maintain your health. While this may seem like odd advice to give to people fighting a serious illness, it sometimes is overlooked. It is vital that you maintain a collaborative relationship with not just your neurologist, but with all your doctors. If you have a question, if something starts to bother you, don't wait. Ask the questions. No one cares more about your health than you do, and if you're not going to fight for it, then you can't expect anyone else to fight for you. In addition, there are proactive steps you can take to make sure your body is in the best condition possible. When facing a challenge everything you do, both psychologically and physically, matters. There are times when we allow one physical challenge to become so overwhelming that we give up on maintaining the rest of our body. It's important to do as much as you can personally but also continue to keep up your regular health regimen. There are almost always things that you can do physically. For some people, just walking a short distance is important; for others, it might be doing basic coordination exercises. I walked.

When I could, I did Pilates. But when physical exercise was difficult, I meditated. In addition to Dr. Weiner, I continued to see other physicians for regular checkups—which, by the way, is how my breast cancer was detected so early. I also followed basic recommendations to encourage good health: I adopted a healthier diet, got plenty of sleep, exercised when I could as I could, and watched my weight.

I didn't choose to be a member of the MS patient community. No one chooses to get a disease or condition. But since that time, I have followed the progress that scientists and physicians have made very closely. Whenever possible I've tried to use the bully pulpit I was given as a governor's wife and then a presidential candidate's wife to attract attention to this disease and advocate for more research. But it wasn't until after the 2012 election that it finally became clear to me how I could make my most important contribution.

Acknowledgments

Many thanks to David Fisher, a kind soul and indispensable collaborator. To my agent, Ellis Trevor, for his guidance through the publishing process. To Kelli Harrison, Leah Malone, and Susan Duprey, for their support in all manner of things. To the team at St. Martin's Press: Laurie Chittenden, a wonderful advocate and editor; publishers Tom Dunne, Sally Richardson, and Pete Wolverton; Tracey Guest, Christy D'Agostini, Laura Clark, Karlyn Hixson, Staci Burt, and all the other superb sales, marketing, and editorial staff, for their excitement and passion for this book. And to Ted Newton and Chris Oman, for sharp editing eyes.

To Drs. Howard Weiner, Dennis Selkoe, and Betsy Nabel, and to the whole Ann Romney Center team for daring to change the world and solve the mysteries of neurologic diseases. I am with you. We are in this together.

To my dear friends, among them Margo Gogan, Beth

Myers, Laraine Wright, and Jan and Amy Ebeling, who agreed to participate in this book and who have been pillars of support. To Stephanie Nielson, an inspiration. To Natalie Crate, dearly missed.

There are others whose names I do not know who nevertheless inspired me beyond measure: They are the women and men suffering from MS and other neurologic diseases who would wait for hours at campaign events to tell me to keep going. I promised you then that hope was on the way, and I will work forevermore to keep that promise. You are my inspiration. I will never forget you.

To all my family—my five amazing sons and daughters-in-law, and all my beautiful grandchildren: I couldn't be a prouder mom and grandma.

Finally, to Mitt: There has been much on this journey I have had to face alone, but you were always there, as you have always been there, for me. You have always believed in me. I have always believed in you.

About the Ann Romney Center for Neurologic Diseases at Brigham and Women's Hospital in Boston, Massachusetts

The Ann Romney Center for Neurologic Diseases at Brigham and Women's Hospital (BWH) is a collaborative global pursuit to accelerate treatments, prevention, and cures for five of the world's most complex neurologic diseases: multiple sclerosis (MS), Alzheimer's disease, ALS (Lou Gehrig's disease), Parkinson's disease, and brain tumors, which affect 50 million people worldwide.

I decided to tell my story hoping that this book would help raise awareness about neurologic diseases. So many people helped and inspired me on this journey; it gives me no greater pleasure than to support the doctors, researchers, staff, and work being done at the Ann Romney Center for Neurologic Diseases.

If you'd like to find out more about the Ann Romney Center for Neurologic Diseases or learn more about how you can help, please visit: www.annromneycenter.org.

If you or a loved one suffers from a neurologic disease and would like to share your story with the more than 50 million people worldwide affected by these devastating diseases, join our community at www.50millionfaces.org.